# SHEFFIELD PUBS

**Barley Corn, Cambridge Street**

The Barley Corn is advertising the Don Brewery's celebrated ales, c. 1901. The pub had been in existence since the late eighteenth century at least, and became tied to A. H. Smith's Don Brewery, Penistone Road (absorbed by Tennant Brothers in 1915), in 1891.

**Sheaf View, Gleadless Road, Heeley**

On 25 February 2000 the *Sheffield Telegraph* stated that the proposed reopening of the Sheaf View pub near Heeley Bottom had been welcomed by the city council. Plans giving the go-ahead included refurbishing and extending the existing empty building and creating a 30-space car park at the corner of Gleadless Road, Prospect Road and Sheaf Bank. Council officers described the premises as 'something of an eyesore at a prominent location close to the edge of the proposed Heeley Millennium Park'. James Birkett, who ran the New Barrack Tavern in Penistone Road, intended to reopen the Sheaf View as a real ale pub.

# SHEFFIELD PUBS

## LANDLORDS AND LANDLADIES

### PETER TUFFREY

FONTHILL

**Punch Bowl, South Street**

The Punch Bowl at 140 South Street, pictured *c.* 1913, may be traced to at least 1822. The premises were acquired by Truswell's Brewery, Eyre Street/Norfolk Lane, in 1894.

**Pack Horse Hotel, West Bar**

Built in 1860, the Pack Horse Hotel is pictured at the junction with Snig Hill, *c.* 1900. Owned by Berry & Co. Breweries from 1870, it was acquired by Sheffield Corporation in 1900 for street improvements and demolished some time later.

FONTHILL MEDIA

www.fonthillmedia.com

First published by Fonthill Media 2012

ISBN 978-1-78155-058-8 (print)

ISBN 978-1-78155-109-7 (e-book)

A CIP catalogue record for this book is available from the British Library

Typeset in 9.5pt on 12pt Mrs Eaves Serif Narrow

Typesetting by Fonthill Media

Printed in the UK

Connect with us

f facebook.com/fonthillmedia  🐦 twitter.com/fonthillmedia

# Introduction

The subject of Sheffield pubs is such a vast and daunting one to tackle, so I have tried to cover it in various ways. The photographs depict pubs over a wide expanse of time – old, new and demolished ones, and those that have existed for a short period with a name change. The pictures not only cover the city centre but also outlying districts.

One of the earliest pictures shows the Pack Horse on Snig Hill. It was a vast building erected to cater for the coaching trade and its balcony was often used by politicians to appear before the electorate and celebrate a victory. Sadly, it was acquired by Sheffield Corporation around 1900 and demolished to facilitate road improvements. Nevertheless, the picture gives us an insight – like many old pictures do – into a world unimaginable today and an area that bears no resemblance to present times.

Many pubs were built to slake the thirsts of steel workers and those in associated trades. There was a proliferation of beer houses and pubs throughout the latter quarter of the eighteenth century and a positive boom through the nineteenth century. Sometimes these were no more than one or two terraced houses knocked together as seen in the pictures of the Prospect Tavern and the Milton Arms. In a number of cases they sat at the corner of rows of terraced houses and provided a unique focal point for a community or works in the area, as seen in the pictures of the Lancers and the Royal George.

Post-war rebuilding in Sheffield after the Blitz in December 1940 was understandably slow. The most dramatic rebuilding as far as pubs were concerned was undoubtedly that of the Marples Hotel, where seventy people lost their lives in the December air raid. For some eighteen years after the incident the area was derelict; at regular intervals flowers were placed on the site by Sheffielders and even John Smith's Brewery as a mark of remembrance before redevelopment took place. Many new pubs were built in the 1950s and 1960s by breweries such as Tennants, Stones, Wards and Tetleys, who had strong interests in the city and surrounding areas.

**The Owl, Neepsend Lane**

On 12 February 1987 the *Star* said that a Sheffield pub with footballing connections had finalised the delayed kick-off for celebrations to mark a revamp and name change. The Owl, which had been appointed as the headquarters for Sheffield Wednesday supporters, planned January 22 festivities, but the date clashed with a wedding party. So the official opening was fixed for 12 February with a free buffet and beer at 50p a pint. Before the soccer link, the pub was known as the Muff Inn, and previously, the Farfield Inn. Manager Steve Gass said: 'We can now offer a home to Wednesday fans who had no permanent base and had to hire rooms where they could. Some are from as far away as Kiveton.' The Owl is pictured here on 17 April 1989.

**Prospect View, Gleadless Road**

Prospect View Hotel, a former Tetley's House, was photographed on 13 February 1976 when William Bearder was the licensee. The pub became part of the Rawson & Company Ltd's tied estate in 1922. In *Pictures of Lost Sheffield Pubs* (1991), J. P. Turley alleges the premises, now demolished, were nicknamed 'the cuckoo'.

Fortunately, as well as finding exterior photographs of pubs, I have also located internal views and these reveal many interesting details – not to mention comparisons to modern interiors – for the observer today. These are aptly shown in pictures of the Sicey, where a village was created in the pub, or the Stonehouse, where there was a courtyard with stocks included. Details are also given of the Tut 'n' Shive, where for a time the pub resembled a builder's yard/rubbish dump just with the aim of pandering to a contemporary trend. Of course, none of these exist today. Also in recent times it is interesting to see how there is a return to the traditional type of real ale boozer as reflected at the Sheaf View, which is just one example.

Sadly, with Sheffield's declining steel industry and a desire by the council to regenerate in certain areas, a great many pubs have been lost, most notably in the Attercliffe area. The Plumpers, right on the eastern edge of the area, is one of the pubs which suffered from declining steelworker trade and was subsequently turned into a golfing shop. The Wellington at Brightside also suffered from lack of trade and extensive road developments and was eventually demolished.

I believe that, for too long, pub books have failed to feature or detail some of antics, eccentricities, tragedies, behaviour or honest hard work of the people who run pubs – the landlords and landladies. For information about their activities I have trawled through literally hundreds of newspapers cuttings from the *Sheffield Star* and *Sheffield Telegraph*.

For the eccentric landlord we would not have to look much further than Dave Bacon at the Staniforth Arms – a keeper of snakes, spiders and goats among other things. And besides running his pub he was also a clown under the name of Mr Potty! I also illustrate pubs where violence has quite dramatically visited the premises: the Viaduct, where the landlady was forced to hand over takings or have her children harmed, the murder at the Nelson and the savage attack at the John O' Gaunt. Of course, some of the older pubs have weird and wonderful ghost stories attached to them – the Queen's Head in the city centre, the Carbrook Hall at Attercliffe, and the Waggon & Horses on Gleadless Road to name but a few. I must admit that one of my favourite landlord/landlady tales concerns Wilfred and Janet Hibbert at the Staffordshire Arms, Sorby Street, where a pickle factory opened in premises adjacent and scattered their regulars. The picture of them standing outside the pub holding their noses is a classic one. The bad luck award must go to Ron Ward at the Crow's Nest Pub, Hyde Park. Ron was dealt a double dose of misfortune as his wife left him for one of his customers, and then the pub owners, Whitbread's Brewery, told him he could not continue as landlord as their policy was that only couples could manage a pub. A fun pub is featured with the Floozy and Firkin – the interior view and the names of the beers will maybe induce some howls of laughter. Interestingly, this pub only lasted a few years and is currently a curry house. A long service story is highlighted with Ron and Beryl Nash at the Victoria Hotel, Penistone Road. The couple were at the pub for twenty-eight years – Ron's dad had also run it before him – until they were forced to quit in 1986 when the site was required for road developments.

Many breweries belched beer fumes across the city during much of the nineteenth and twentieth centuries. Where possible I have tried to give details about brewery ownership of pubs. Potted histories with pictures of three breweries – the Exchange Brewery, Hope & Anchor Brewery, and William Stones Brewery – may be found within these pages.

Besides newspaper cuttings, I have also found the following books of use: *South Yorkshire Stingo A Directory of South Yorkshire Brewers 1758-1795* by David Lloyd Parry; *Pictures of Lost Sheffield Pubs* by J. P. Turley; *The definitive A to Z listing of Sheffield Public Houses* by Michael Liversidge; and *A Pub On Every Corner* by Douglas Lamb. Mention must also be made of the excellent website www.sheffieldhistory.co.uk which is the product of much painstaking research by contributors to provide an index of Sheffield pubs.

I hope you find this book as satisfying to read as I have in gathering the information and pictures for its production. Special thanks to Sheffield Newspapers, particularly Stuart Hastings, Paul License and Jane Salt. Gratitude is also due to my son Tristram for his research and help with the text. I would also like to thank Hugh Parkin for his help and support as always. If you would like to make any comments on the text or pictures please make contact via email: petertuffrey@rocketmail.com or by post Peter Tuffrey, 8 Wrightson Avenue, Warmsworth, Doncaster South Yorks, DN4 9QL.

Peter Tuffrey
September 2012

**Arbourthorne Hotel, Errington Road, Manor**
Pictured pulling the first pints at the official opening of the Arbourthorne Hotel after refurbishment early in December 1984 are, from left to right: Mel Stirland, Gary Shelton (Sheffield Wednesday), Josie and Terry Fisher (landlady and landlord), Charlie Williamson (Sheffield Wednesday) and Russell Black (Sheffield United).

## Adelphi Hotel, Arundel Street

The premises, dating from at least 1849, were the venue for the formation of Yorkshire County Cricket Club on 8 January 1863 and Sheffield Wednesday Football Club in 1867. Henry Sampson who ran the pub during the mid-nineteenth century was also noted for his cricketing capabilities. The pub was sold by Chambers' Brunswick Brewery to William Stones' Brewery in February 1912. Tom Bolton was landlord from the late 1920s to the 1940s and was dubbed 'the sporting landlord' by the *Star* in his obituary in 1962. The *Star* of 6 February 1993 noted: 'Before he entered the pub trade he had a colourful career as an amateur and professional boxer. He was also a footballer with Mexborough Town, Gainsborough Trinity, Rotherham Town and West Ham United and an amateur cricketer.' The *Sheffield Telegraph* of Thursday 29 May 1969 stated that 'the Adelphi Hotel closed its doors for the last time last night.' The newspaper also explained that it was being demolished so that its site on Tudor Way, opposite the Lyceum, 'can be freed for redevelopment.' At lunchtime, Wednesday officials and Yorkshire stars, led by Norman Yardley, had gathered there to say goodbye to their birthplace. The Adelphi had close connections with both the Lyceum and the Old Theatre Royal, which was destroyed by fire in December 1935, and had handbills for the Royal dating back many years. The landlord, 55-year-old, John Costello and wife Ann, were leaving to take over a new pub, the Toll Gate, Pitsmoor. Compensation totalling around £19,000 to the owners of the Adelphi was approved by the City Council Town Planning Committee.

**The Albert, Division Street/Cambridge Street**

The Albert pub, on the Division Street/Cambridge Street corner, can be traced to at least 1797 when it was called Union. It was renamed Albert to commemorate the death of Prince Albert.

**The Albert, Division Street/Cambridge Street**

The Albert is pictured during demolition – 8-10 November 1979 – the building having been declared unstable. The site subsequently became a car park before Whitbread announced in April 1998 that redevelopment would take place. The RSVP bar and then Yates's bar have since occupied the site.

### Bell Hagg Inn/John Thomas, Manchester Road

The *Sheffield Star* of 11 May 1996 reported that after landlord John Chidlaw took over the Bell Hagg (formerly known as Hodgson's Folly) in 1965, he decided to rename the pub after his grandfather, John Thomas. However, objections were raised by a conservation group and officers from the council's planning department told him that the signs had to be removed as they were 'considered to be obtrusive and detrimental to the amenities of the locality'. The head of Sheffield Council's development control was adamant that the name change wasn't the problem, but John Chidlaw thought that its rude connotation was the main reason behind the complaints. The pub later reverted back to its original name. Former owners included A. H. Smith's Don Brewery. Both pictures were taken on 17 November 1981.On www.closedpubs.co.uk it is stated that the pub was built in 1832 and had five floors. It is currently in ruins.

## Big Tree, Chesterfield Road

Sheffield had its first Brewburger on 27 October 1982 when an American-style burger restaurant and pub opened in what used to be the Big Tree pub (also known as the Mason's Arms from at least 1825 and rebuilt in 1901). It was the second Brewburger in the area for Whitbread's who already had one at Wickersley. The brewery had invested £100,000 in the venture, creating six full-time and fifteen part-time jobs in the process. The design was the work of Whitbread's own Sheffield-based architects and interior design department. The pub-restaurant was to be managed jointly by Miss Yorkshire Television, Jill Saxby, and her fiancé Peter Yates. In November 1995 the big tree outside the pub was felled due to disease. Manager Bill Barton is seen with a cross-section of the tree. Among the former owners of the pub were Strout's Brewery and Tennant Brothers.

### Black Swan, Snig Hill

During the Sheffield Blitz the main bars of the Black Swan (dating from the late eighteenth century) were reduced to rubble. However, this did not deter the landlord who converted his private rooms for use by the pub's customers; this was the situation for the next twenty-one years until the site was redeveloped. The new Black Swan, built along with office accommodation, reopened almost exactly twenty-three years after the Sheffield Blitz, on 11 December 1963. The pub later became famous as a music venue, hosting acts such as Joe Cocker, Dr Feelgood, the Clash and the Sex Pistols. Later name changes included Compleat Angler, Mucky Duck and the Boardwalk.

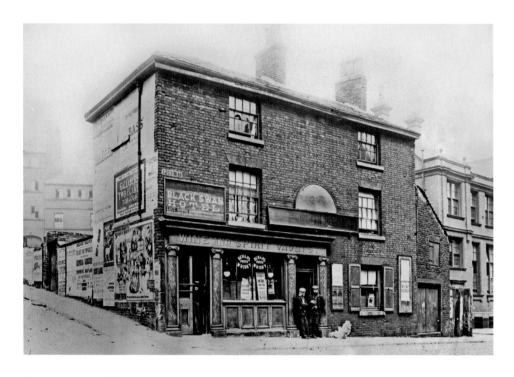

**Black Swan, Pond Street**

Dating from at least 1822, the Black Swan, Pond Street (once known as Little Pond Street), is seen here in *c.* 1901. At one time the premises were tied to Richdale's Britannia Brewery, Bramall Lane. On the right is the General Post Office.

**Blue Ball, Main Road, Wharncliffe**

The Blue Ball, dating from at least 1833, is pictured here in *c.* 1916 when William Young was the landlord. A list of the pub's past landlords reveals that Young was there for only a brief period.

**Brown Bear Norfolk Street**

The Brown Bear, a Grade II listed building located on Norfolk Street, dates from at least 1822, and according to David Parry in 1997, George Beet 'brewed here in the late 1870s'. Located near to the Town Hall and both the Crucible and Lyceum Theatres, the Brown Bear has gained a reputation for attracting politicians, theatre-goers and even the occasional actor. Brown Bear landlord Martin Smith is pictured on 27 November 1995.

**Brown Bear, Norfolk Street**

The Brown Bear was bought by Sheffield Corporation in the 1930s, and when the lease was up for renewal in 1981 a stipulation was included that the character of the pub could not be altered. The winning bidder for the lease was John Smith's brewery, who had been lease-holders since 1955. The premises were later run by Samuel Smith's and are pictured here on 17 November 1972.

**Brewer on the Bridge, Bridge Street**

In 1979 the Brewer on the Bridge underwent a £70,000 refurbishment and made national television and newspaper reports for allegedly turning away regular customers. It was claimed that the owners, Whitbread, were trying to raise the reputation of the pub, which was formerly known as Lady's Bridge. A spokesman for Whitbread was quoted: 'We welcome all our old and new customers equally, provided that everybody conforms to the generally accepted standards of behaviour in a pub.' New landlord Knud Jensen, posing in front of the premises on 12 November 1980, had previously been a consultant with a hotel company in the West Indies, which had catered for the Queen during her visit to Barbados. He was hoping to apply his skills to the cuisine on offer at the pub. The premises closed in 1993.

**Bull's Head, Fullwood Road, Ranmoor**

The Bull's Head football team made headlines for the wrong reasons on 13 January 1992. The *Star* reported that the team had been assaulted while playing a Sunday League tie against the Highway pub team. Midfielder David Sweetman was assaulted three times and kicked unconscious in front of his wife, who was watching from the sidelines. He needed hospital treatment and could not work. Police had to be called to allow the Bull's Head players to leave safely. Referee Derek Taylor was quoted as saying '[the match was] one of the worst experiences I've had in 25 years.' A Bull's Head player said: 'When one lad was booked for smoking during the match I knew this was not going to be a normal game. The level of violence and numbers involved really sickened me.' The pub was part of Richdale's Britannia Brewery tied estate from 1875.

**Burgoyne Arms, Langsett Road**

The *Star* reported on 22 December 1980 that the children of the Sacred Heart Children's Home would have some Christmas presents thanks to the regulars at the Burgoyne Arms, Hillsborough. Money for the presents was raised from the pub swear-box, conker competitions and donations. The total raised was £432. Landlord Trevor Oates said that everyone that had come into the pub had contributed in some way. He added: 'We got £102 from the swear-box alone and that's mainly from one bunch we call the "Nutter's Club".' City stores joined in the festive spirit by giving discounts on the gifts, which included a television, video game, board games, football nets and a £10 gift certificate for each child. The pub, dating from at least 1852, is pictured on 14 December 1977. In 1860 Robert Hales – the Norfolk Giant – was noted as landlord at the Burgoyne Arms.

**But 'n' Ben, Howard Street**

'A change of name an impressive refurbishment and one of Sheffield's premier gay pubs ... became the But 'n' Ben,' reported the *Sheffield Star* of 12 April 1995. Before switching to its unusual name, this was the Cossack pub.

**Byards Leap, Daresbury Drive**

Of all the Sheffield pubs, the name of this one probably has the strangest stories behind it. Allegedly, 300 years ago, a young girl sold herself to the devil for power over the people and things of the district where she lived. Her looks departed her and she became increasingly wicked every day. The people in the area knew her as 'Old Meg' and an old soldier called 'Black Jim' vowed to kill her. When he went to her hut she flew out at him and dug her talons into the flanks of the horse he was riding (called Byard) and lifted it over 300 yards in four leaps. Black Jim then thrust his sword into Old Meg's heart killing her, ridding the area of the misfortune she brought. The choice of this name for a pub in Sheffield is also strange as Byard's Leap is a hamlet in the North Kesteven district of Lincolnshire. H. Killingbeck, from William Stones Brewery, who chose the name, told the *Sheffield Telegraph* of 17 November 1964 that Byards Leap was picked because he was looking for something unusual.

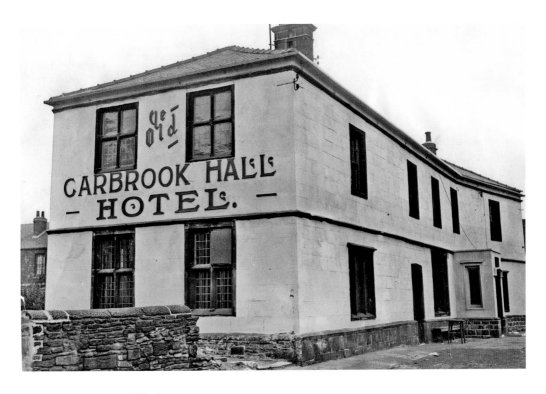

**Carbrook Hall, Attercliffe Common**

According to a new book reviewed in the *Star* on 26 October 1983, Carbrook Hall was one of the most haunted houses in Sheffield. The ghosts said to inhabit the premises included an old Edwardian lady, an old man, a hooded monk and a Roundhead in a black hat (a smoker, as he was said to stand next to the cigarette machine). They perpetrated a number of strange incidents including glasses thrown from shelves, televisions turned off, drawers dislodged, floating cigarettes and people grabbed by unseen hands. Landlord and landlady Keith and Doreen Moorhouse, pictured here, were quick to dismiss these claims as, in the year they had been resident, they had not had any problems.

*Fireplace . Carbrook old Hall*

**Carbrook Hall, Attercliffe Common**

The original Carbrook Hall dates from the twelfth century when it was in the hands of the Blunt Family. This was rebuilt in 1462, and in the seventeenth century it passed to the Bright family; it was later used by John Bright for meetings of the Parliamentarians during the Civil War. Most of the building was demolished in the nineteenth century and what survives is a Grade II listed stone wing that was added *c.* 1620. It became a pub during the mid-nineteenth century and has since gained Grade II listed status due to the historical interest of some of the features such as the carved oak panelling and plaster work of the ceiling.

*Above left:* **Carlisle Hotel, Carlisle Street East**

Men were barred from behind the Carlisle Hotel bar during the early 1990s as two sisters-in-law were firmly in charge. The *Sheffield Star* of 5 October 1991 reported that Betty and Vera Leigh had just become the landladies of the Carlisle Hotel, with Betty fulfilling a lifelong ambition to run a pub. The Carlisle Hotel, dating from at least the 1850s, was in the news the following year after the success of Country music nights held there. The premises, formerly tied to William Stones Ltd, have also been titled Ma Bakers/Ave-it-Bar. The photograph is reproduced courtesy of John Law.

*Above right:* **Cavell's, High Street**

The *Star* announced on 17 August 1995 that the Old Blue Bell had undergone a transformation to become Cavell's cafe and bar. Owner of the premises in both its guises, Brian Thorlby, was pleased with the alteration to a continental-themed premises, as he admitted that the Old Blue Bell was a bit of a dive. Brian, pictured with his son Dean, was also a DJ while landlord at the Old Blue Bell and was known under the name Brian Cavell. While son Dean managed the bar, Brian also turned his hand to chef duties, cooking breakfast and chargrilled chicken. The refurbishment cost £200,000 and included a £10,000 coffee machine.

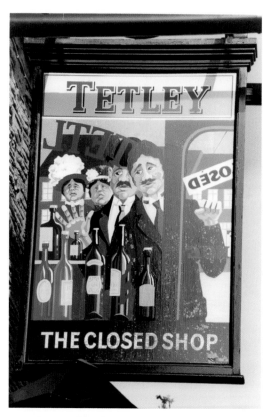

### Closed Shop, Commonside, Walkley

Mystery surrounded the unspecified closure of the Closed Shop in Walkley at the start of June 1963. The *Sheffield Telegraph* reported that the barman, Harold Bunting, had turned up for work only to find all the doors locked and no sign of the landlord, Mr Colin Fletcher. Mr Bunting enquired to neighbours who said they had seen Mr Fletcher drive away in his van. When the brewery and police gained entry to the premises it was found that all of the landlord's clothes and personal belongings had gone. The article also revealed that Mr Fletcher's wife and two daughters had left two weeks earlier. The *Sheffield Star* of 2 July 1963 then reported that a transfer of the licence had been granted from Mr Fletcher to Phillip Mulvaney. Mr Fletcher was found at a Castleton hotel and was quoted as saying: 'I have finished with the licensing trade. All I want to do is start afresh.' The picture of the pub exterior dates from 6 June 1963.

**Closed Shop, Commonside, Walkley**

In contrast to the previous story, Closed Shop landlord and landlady Harry and Lee Watson, pictured on 14 October 1995, clearly enjoyed their time at the pub. They had been there for four years when the *Star's* 'Pub Call' feature of 25 October 1995 praised the pub's cosy and welcoming atmosphere and traditional decor. The pub once belonged to Duncan Gilmour & Co. Ltd's tied estate.

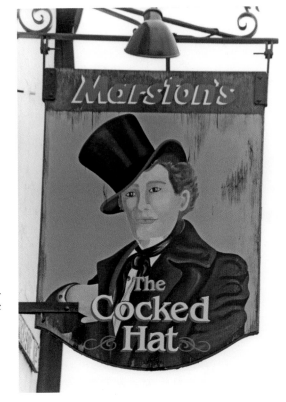

**Cocked Hat, Worksop Road**

A Cocked Hat fundraiser was reported to be making history on 27 July 1990. Landlord Alec Robshaw asked City Morris Dancers to perform on the green adjacent to the pub to raise money for the Deerlands Special School. One of the dancers, Mike Wild, informed Alec that it could possibly be the first time that Morris dancing had taken place on the green in around 160 years. The event was captured for posterity and more events were planned for the raising of funds for the school.

**Cocked Hat, Worksop Road**

A triple celebration was staged at the end of May 1995 at the Cocked Hat. The first involved landlord Alec Robshaw (62) and his wife Ethel (61) after they announced they would enter semi-retirement in July. Alec had been in the trade for thirty-five years and was previously President of the Sheffield Licensed Victuallers Association. Regulars were assured that the pub would stay the same as the reins were handed over to their son Antony. Money was also presented to the Sheffield Wheelchair Sports Club as events organised by the pub had raised £366. To cap the celebrations, the Cocked Hat was included in the CAMRA Good Pub Guide for the tenth year running under the direction of Alec, which was a rare achievement. The pub is seen here on 4 November 1981.

**Cocked Hat, Worksop Road**

Antony Robshaw was featured in the *Star's* Pub Call feature on 17 February 1999, and it was reported that he was keeping the traditions set out by his parents before they retired. The pub was included in the CAMRA Good Pub Guide for the thirteenth year and Antony had notched up further awards. The Cocked Hat was named CAMRA pub of the month for Sheffield and Antony received the national Cask Marque for keeping ale at a consistent standard. Antony, Ethel and Alec Robshaw are pictured here on 27 April 1993.

**Compleat Angler, Snig Hill**

The barmaid of the Compleat Angler (formerly Black Swan) probably wished she had gone fishing after her charity parachute jump went wrong in April 1982. Eileen Benton, along with other pub staff, parachuted in aid of the Lodge Moor Hospital spinal unit. Eileen came to earth with a bump and landed in hospital herself with a suspected broken leg. The jump claimed another victim in DJ Barry White, who sprained an ankle.

**Compleat Angler, Snig Hill**

Another mishap befell a member of the Compleat Angler bar staff and was reported in the *Sheffield Telegraph* of 28 June 1984. Head Barman Philip Ogle was preparing the bar for opening and went to the kitchen downstairs to get ice. While he was in the room the self-locking door slammed shut and he was unable to get out as he had left his keys in the bar. Unwilling to miss opening time he asked the staff in the Old Brewery Taps to send him back upstairs in the dumb waiter, which the pubs shared. Philip got in with the ice and when he reached the top found that the doors were jammed shut. He then tried to return to the kitchen but found the lift had stopped working. His cries for help could be heard in the Old Brewery Taps and the staff called the fire brigade to get him out.

**Connelly's, Main Road, Darnall**
'The Irish theme pub explosion continues unabated,' announced the *Star* on 27 March 1996. The latest recruit was the former Rose & Crown in Darnall. The *Star* reported that even Ward's Brewery admitted that this pub was not the most inviting before gaining a new lease of life as Connelly's. As the Rose & Crown, it apparently had something of a bad reputation, but as Connelly's it was putting the past behind it and attracting new regulars. Leaseholder Gail Connelly, from whom the pub took its name, said: 'Visitors are really impressed with the new bar's look'. Landlady Mrs Dot Dunkeirt is seen at the pub on 25 March 1996.

**Cricketer's Arms, Bramall Lane**
The pub can be traced to at least 1859 and was acquired by William Stones in 1916. The photograph was taken on 7 April 1983.

**Cricketer's Arms, Bramall Lane**

Tony and Eleanor Howard behind the bar at the Cricketer's Arms, Bramall Lane, on 25 May 1988.

**Old Cross Daggers, Market Square, Woodhouse**

In August 1970 the end was near for the Old Cross Daggers pub at Woodhouse; it was to serve its last pint on the 26th. The regulars were far from pleased and were fighting to keep the old pub from closing. They had a petition with over 250 signatures, which they were going to present to Sheffield Council. A spokesman for Joshua Tetley & Son, owners of the pub, said the pub was no longer economically viable and given the large amount of money needed to bring it up to modern standards the best course of action was to close the premises. The locals had been trying to stop the closure for the past four years. The photograph dates from 23 January 1966.

**Cross Daggers Restaurant, Market Square**

The *Sheffield Telegraph* of 6 December 1971 reported that the pub was to reopen but as a restaurant under the guidance of caterer Richard Margetts. In the following May, a new guard dog at the Old Cross Daggers restaurant was almost looking for a new career less than 24 hours after its first one had began. Jason the dog was fast asleep and snoring loudly as a thief struck in the next room, pushing over employee Vera Leonard and escaping with £7 from a cash box. Manageress Miss Wendy Crossley commented to the *Star:* 'We have been telling everyone we have this guard dog, but he's just like a little baby and he's still on milk feeds. We were told he might cause a few restless nights, but he sleeps most of the time.' It was noted that Jason was to be given a second chance.

**Cross Keys, Handsworth Road**

'There's a rumour in Handsworth that a secret tunnel links the Cross Keys pub with Sheffield's Manor Castle, a mile or so away,' claimed the *Star* of 18 April 1988. But landlord Frank Francis-Taylor (pictured in the lounge, formerly the landlord's private quarters) didn't believe it. He said the lie of the land was all wrong. When he retired in 1990, after fifteen years behind the bar, it would bring to an end a long family tradition at the Cross Keys. He married Connie, widow of the previous landlord, whose father, Joe Francis, held the tenancy before him from the early 1930s.

### Cross Keys, Handsworth Road

After a £100,000 refurbishment of the pub in August 1991, it was reported that a novel way of attracting new customers was being tried by Terry and Judy Spalding, who had taken over the pub the previous year. Six hundred balloons were released containing a message from the pub and a voucher for a free drink at the pub. Great care had been taken during renovations to protect the cask conditioned William Stones, which was a favourite of real ale enthusiasts. The picture was taken on 12 August 1969.

### Cross Scythes, Baslow Road, Totley

In April 1988 a second War of the Roses erupted in Totley. Landlord Paul Harrison of the Cross Scythes, a Lancastrian, had declared war with Yorkshireman John Dawson, landlord of the neighbouring Fleur de Lys. Both had assembled an army and were ready to do battle on May Day, all in the name of charity, of course. This included a tug of war, barrel push and drinking a yard of ale. Paul Harrison told the *Star* of 25 April 1988, 'Those fellas at the Flirty Flea don't stand a chance as I've got my army training and eating raw meat ... I've sent them an official declaration of war and told them they are in for a thrashing, but they haven't replied to the challenge.'

**Cross Scythes, Baslow Road, Totley**

The *Star* of 10 December 1983 announced that the Cross Scythes would close in the new year for two months, to be turned into an old world carvery. The alterations were to make the premises Whitbread's first Roast Inn Carvery serving traditional meals in Sheffield. But the regulars were not being forgotten. The Cross Scythes would still be a pub once the changes were complete. Whitbread had a number of Roast Inns located in the south and had decided to bring the idea north. The premises date back to at least 1818, and were once part of the Tennant Bros tied estate.

**Cross Inn, Woodfall Lane, Low Bradfield**

The pub dates from around 1865 and became tied to A. H. Smith & Co.'s Don Brewery from 1880. The premises closed *c.* 1978 and have been converted to a private house. Pictured in the doorway is licensee, Francis Wilson's wife, Ann. The couple were at the inn during the last decade of the nineteenth century.

**The Cross Scythes, Derbyshire Lane**

Terry and Elaine Baggaley at the Cross Scythes pub, Derybshire Lane, 14 September 2001. The pub dates back to at least 1825, and was formerly tied to Duncan Gilmour & Co. Ltd.

**Crosspool Tavern, Manchester Road**

In November 1995 it was announced the Crosspool Tavern, once part of Truswell's tied estate, would undergo a £180,000 refurbishment. Owners Toby Restaurants were to improve the bar and restaurant by extending a balcony and increasing seating.

**Crown Inn, Forncett Street**
The pub dates from at least 1871. The photograph was taken on 17 July 1990 and the premises have since closed. The property has been converted for use as offices by a building company.

**Crosspool Tavern, Manchester Road**
Pictured on 6 April 1996 are (left to right) hosts Tracey and Simon Hollands, and Licensee Katy Price. The 'Pub Call' feature in the *Sheffield Star* of 10 April praised a refurbishment for keeping the character of the pub intact. Also praised was the switch to a non-smoking environment. The move was approved by the Health Authority and National Asthma Campaign; subsequently it was awarded the Roy Castle Clean Air Award.

### Crown and Glove, Uppergate, Stannington

The World Cup was given the red card by Crown and Glove landlord Keith Ravenhall in June 1998. He was followed by a number of other landlords in not showing any action from the tournament. Keith told the *Star* of 11 June 1998, 'There will be no telly and I'm not bringing one in. It's the sort of pub that doesn't have a jukebox, pin table, pool table or one-armed bandit, [it's] a place to have a quiet chat.' He added that customers were free to talk about the tournament if they wished.

### Crown Inn, Hillfoot Road, Totley

A nice bird became a regular at the Crown Inn, Totley, the *Star* reported in November 1977. But it wasn't the kind that the regulars would have hoped for, as the bird in question was a blue tit. Landlord John Harrop explained that the bird nested in the tree opposite the pub and when the nights began to get colder it would come over to the pub to sleep above the 'opening time' lamp to keep warm. This was the second year that the bird had frequented the pub. John said: 'I have noticed that it has become quite a habit with customers that, as they walk up they look up to see if the bird is there before coming in.' The exterior of the Crown was photographed on 20 April 1973.

*Above left:* **Crown Inn, Totley**

Landlord of the Crown Inn, John Harrop, is pictured with his wife Sandra on 17 February 1981. The couple had been at the Crown Inn for four years and had previously been at the South Seas pub in Broomhill. They replaced licensees Jack and Evelyn Taylor who had been at the pub for fifteen years when they retired in August 1976.

*Above right:* **Crow's Nest, Hyde Park**

Landlord Ron Ward had the tables turned on him when he was left crying into his pint at the Crow's Nest, Hyde Park, in 1975. Ron was dealt a double dose of misfortune as his wife left him for one of his customers, then the owners of the pub, Whitbread's Brewery, told him he could not continue as landlord as their policy was that only couples could manage a pub. The regulars of the pub rallied round him in his time of need and were organising a petition to hand to the brewery. Ron said: 'I did have my suspicions but did not think it would go this far ... She says she has fallen in love with him and won't be coming back.' The *Star* of 18 March 1975 reported that the 1,000-name-strong petition had failed and Ron was informed that he and his two children had to vacate the pub. Ron thanked everyone for their support and was looking for another job. He said he would stay in the trade if he could.

**Dallas Bar, Fife Street**

The clientele of the Dallas Bar in Wincobank were said to causing a nuisance to local residents in March 1983 (the date of the picture) and this was given as the reason for the refusal for a renewal of the pub's licence. It was reported that locals had seen fights, people having sex in the street and urinating on doorsteps after closing time at the pub. There was also objections raised to the noise created by this 'fun' pub. Licensee Joseph Pratt said he would appeal and it was reported by the *Sheffield Telegraph* of 25 June 1983 that he had been successful. The court was told that the police and environmental health officers had no objections to the renewal and a private investigator also found no evidence of bad behaviour when watching closing time at the pub. The pub, formerly the Engineers (and once tied to Thomas Berry's Moorhead Brewery), closed in January 1985 but re-opened as Barrow House. It has subsequently been demolished.

**Denison Arms, Watery Street**

In August 1991, landlady Wendy Barnes became a casualty of recent cutbacks by Bass Brewery who were to sell the Denison Arms, dating back to at least the mid-nineteenth century. The brewery blamed the decision on the Government as 2,000 pubs had to be sold by the company as part of MMC recommendations. Wendy had been at the pub for a successful six years, making it a favourite of real ale enthusiasts. The pub had become part of the Truswell Brewery's tied estate in 1866.

**Devonshire Arms, South Street/Herries Road**

The Devonshire began life near the foot of the Moor and can be traced to a least 1825. Parry (1997) notes that John Cadman was brewing on the premises in 1854 and William Stacey succeeded him in 1862. The pub was flattened in the Blitz of 1940 but re-opened in a prefab in Herries Road during June 1949. In 1962 new premises were built. The picture above shows the original pub after the Blitz.

**Devonshire Arms, South Street/Herries Road**

On 10 September 1973 the *Star* stated: 'Bernard's a pretty troublesome regular at the Devonshire Arms. But no-one ever tries to throw him out. For Bernard is a ghost.' He was famous among bar staff and customers alike for providing such entertaining diversions as ripping cigar racks from the walls, knocking wine bottles out of their racks and turning off the beer taps! Landlord Dennis Wilson who had been at the pub since it opened eleven years earlier said: 'He likes a drop of gin. On some nights I have measured the optics in the gin bottle – next morning three or four measures have gone. That is too much to have been lost by condensation and no-one else has had it.' The prefab building is seen above on 10 June 1949.

**Devonshire Arms, South Street/Herries Road**

Head barman Michael Austin said the following about Bernard the ghost: 'On a number of occasions the beer has stopped coming through. When I went down the cellar the taps had been turned off but there was nobody there. If the taps had not been set correctly the flow of beer could turn them off so to make sure we tied the taps ... and it still happened.' The final proof of Bernard's existence was provided by Neil Franklyn. He had seen him – standing in the lounge bar drinking. 'Bernard was supposed to be the ghost of the man who had the pub built, and should have been the first manager. He died five months before its completion,' informed the *Star*. The premises were extensively refurbished and a glass conservatory was added in 1987. The picture of the new pub was taken on 8 November 1988.

**Devonshire Arms, High Street, Dore**

Steve and Doreen Jones, pictured, took over the reins at the Devonshire Arms, Dore, in March 1994. The couple came from the Devonshire Arms on Ecclesall Road. Steve had previously been a car salesman, while Doreen had been a roaming national sales boss. They said their reason for changing careers was they wanted to do something different. Another option they thought about was running a fish and chip shop. Steve added: 'I fancied a pub for the same reason everybody else does – you can drink for nothing and spend all day socialising.' After a year of training he realised this was not what running a pub was about but they had no regrets about their decision.

## Devonshire Arms, Dore

Steve and Doreen Jones presided over a refurbishment of the pub (said to date from 1771) in 1994, which kept its character intact. The main feature of this was the new restaurant with dedicated kitchen staff and an emphasis on traditional food. The Devonshire Arms was formerly tied to the Old Albion Brewery on Ecclesall Road. The *Sheffield Telegraph* of 11 December 1998 reported that when he was not at work in the pub, landlord Tony Warburton could be found either working as the school crossing warden or raising money for charity. His latest money raising event saw him spending eight hours on a basketball court trying to get 2,000 baskets in that time. He was hoping to raise £2,500 for permanent all-weather basketball facilities in Dore. In the event Tony did it in seven and a half hours but at a price: 'The joints in my elbow are aching, but what's surprising is my calves with all that going up on tiptoe. I feel like an old man, but it's for a good cause.'

**Devonshire Arms, Ecclesall Road**

The end of July 1986 witnessed two celebrations for Devonshire Arm landlord, Wilf Carlin, and his wife Lucy. The first saw Wilf become Ward's Brewery's longest serving landlord, clocking up twenty-seven years with them. He had been at the Devonshire Arms for twelve years, arriving from the Royal Oak at Hollis Croft where he had spent fifteen years. The second was for the pub being named CAMRA Pub of the Year for its traditional ales and traditional decor. Wilf said: 'We've no other entertainments. We've always been noted for the pint. That's what people want. We have a laugh with our regulars, kidding them on a bit. We don't charge for insults.'

Wilf and Lucy Carlin retired a year later in September 1987 and were succeeded by Bill and Anne Stanaway, formerly of the Red House in Solly Street. The pub was heavily refurbished by Ward's, however, it still retained its traditional character when reopened in April 1989. The pub was also going to retain its focus on traditional ales, but it was attempting to build up a similar reputation for traditional pub food. Bill and Anne had already honed the reputation at the Red House with an upcoming entry for those premises in the CAMRA Good Pub Food Guide. The speciality was Anne's giant Yorkshire puddings with onion gravy and filling of choice. The picture on the left was taken on 14 April 1989. The one on the right of Wilf and Lucy Carlin was taken on 24 July 1986.

**Devonshire Arms, Ecclesall Road**

Two interesting discoveries were made by builders when the pub was undergoing refurbishment. The first happened in 1975 when the *Star* of 8 March reported that a well had been uncovered in the garden where new toilets were to be built. A sign said it had been covered in 1907 by R.M.S., later found to be previous landlord Robert Marshall Scott. The 25-feet-deep well was ordered to be filled in. During the work of the late 1980s, a second discovery was made – this one being that the pub had no foundations. The gable ends had to be taken down, the building underpinned and then rebuilt. The above photograph of the bar was taken on 14 April 1989.

**Devonshire Cat, Wellington Street**

The Fat Cat pub at Kelham Island was to have a kitten, announced the *Sheffield Telegraph* of 6 October 2000. The new pub, the Devonshire Cat, was to be built as part of a new student flats complex on Wellington Street in the Devonshire Quarter. The venture was headed by businessman David Wickett, who also owned the Kelham Island Brewery and Fat Cat. The pub was to specialise in real ale.

**The Domino, Egerton Street**

The *Star* of 20 May 1970 announced that a new pub would be serving the locals of the Broomhall area. This was the Domino built by Sheffield Corporation as part of the Broomhall development with the flats seen to the rear. The pub was designed by Hadfield, Cawkwell, Davidson & Partners and the construction work was carried out by Osborn Furness Ltd of Sheffield. The pub, seen here on 3 May 1984, was leased to Ward's Brewery by the Corporation, with the brewery giving them the Scarborough Arms, Milton Street, in return. The interior was designed by Robin More Ede of London.

**The Domino, Egerton Street**

Pictured on 3 May 1984 is Domino landlord Alan Simpson. In the 1980s, the Broomhall flats were demolished and subsequently replaced by more housing. The pub has since been transformed into student accommodation.

**Dore Moor Inn, Hathersage Road, Dore**
In July 1994, the Dore Moor Inn was noted as leading the way for the visually impaired by providing menus dedicated for their use. The pub provided three menus – one in Braille, one with large print, and a talking menu. It was hoped this would let poorly sighted people retain their independence. The pub was once part of Henry Tomlinson's Anchor Brewery tied estate.

**Dog & Partridge, Attercliffe Road**
From 1853 the pub was tied to Bentley's Old Brewery. It has also been known as Goodfellas Gentlemans' Club.

**Dove & Rainbow, Hartshead**
The *Sheffield Telegraph* of 15 July 1957 presented a nostalgic feature on the Dove & Rainbow as it was to be demolished and the licence transferred to a new building in close proximity. It was said to be a popular spot for recruiting men for the Army and Navy during the latter half of the eighteenth century and many men had been enlisted after visiting the premises. Another concerned a vicar with an unusual skill. Revd James Wilkinson, a man with a strong physique, heart and mind, was dining in the pub when two men came in wanting to test his boxing skills. The vicar took the men outside into the yard and gave both a sound thrashing before finishing his meal. The pub, pictured on 13 July 1957, was also well known for being frequented by journalists and lawyers.

**Dove & Rainbow, Hartshead**

When the pub moved it took the bottom floor of a new four-storey building constructed as part of the redevelopment of Hartshead and Watson's Walk. The pub had a central bar which served two rooms that were panelled in grey sycamore and cedar. The building was designed by M. Oldfield of Tennants Brothers, while the building work was carried out mainly by A. Bradbury & Sons Ltd. The new landlord was Maurice Jones, who replaced the landlady of the old premises, Mrs Elizabeth Grayson.

**Earl Grey, Ecclesall Road**

Barmaid Sandra Winter was celebrating in June 1978 after winning a Barmaid of the Year competition. She beat 500 other hopefuls to the title awarded by a national newspaper. Sandra, 24, said the secret of her success was 'being able to smile, no matter what.' She added: 'I love meeting people and I always try to be pleasant and chatty.' Part of her prize was a holiday to Barbados, which she was to go on with husband Patrick. She had her brother Michael to thank for entering her in the competition. The picture was taken on 16 November 1979.

### Earl Grey, Ecclesall Road

The *Sheffield Gazette* of 7 April 1983 announced that the Earl Grey would be a victim of the bulldozer as part of a £625,000 scheme to widen Ecclesall Road. The section between Moore Street and Pear Street was to be made into a dual carriageway and would also see the demise of the New Inn. The history of the pub may be traced to at least 1833 and among the past owners were Tennant Brothers. The photograph dates from 24 May 1978.

### Earl Marshal, East Bank Road

The Earl Marshal was the second incarnation for this building as it had previously been the Midhill Working Men's Club. It closed in July 1983 amid mounting debts, continued losses and alleged bad management. There was no question of it reopening as a club as the owners, Ward's Brewery, saw no future in this and the only alternative was to reopen as a pub, which it did in May 1984 as the Earl Marshal. The premises underwent a £80,000 refurbishment, including the restoration of an old estate house that formed part of the building. The interior featured three interestingly themed lounges – a colonial room, Victorian room and garden party room.

**Earl Marshal, East Bank Road**

Taking over the new pub were Alan and Pat Gough, pictured on 15 May 1984. Alan, 38, had previously been a sergeant in the Parachute Regiment and had a stint in the Merchant Navy. The couple, originally from Middlesbrough, were going to divide responsibilities; Alan the bar and managing the staff, and Pat the catering. The couple had been in the trade for eight years, moving from Wakefield for this, their fifth pub. They had been in Sheffield previously to manage the Richmond Hotel.

**Empire Bar, Charter Square**

The *Sheffield Telegraph* of 22 August 1997 announced that the Empire Bar, Charter Square, had been given the go-ahead by magistrates. The bar was to have outdoor and indoor seating for 600 and an interior based on Hollywood film sets. £500,000 was being spent on the project, which was due to open in October 1997. Entrepreneur and partner in the scheme, Mo Tanwir said: 'Sheffield hasn't seen anything like this yet. We are trying to make it a little more like London and create a more continental atmosphere.'

**Empire Bar, Charter Square**
Rachel Calvert, licensee at the Empire Bar, is pictured during January 2001.

**Exchange Brewery, Bridge Street**
A view inside Sheffield's Exchange Brewery, Bridge Street, on the 30 January 1963. In the foreground, the Brew House foreman, Mr Arthur Atkins, takes the temperature of boiling beer in the coppers. In the background, Mr George Elvin is adding hops to one of the coppers as part of the brewing process.

**Exchange Brewery Bridge Street**
Exchange Brewery workers are pictured rolling a mixture of old and new barrels that are to be delivered to various pubs. The picture was taken on 6 July 1962.

**Exchange Brewery, Bridge Street**
The Exchange brewery was founded by Samuel Cheatle Proctor and originally located close to Sheffield Corn Exchange. He was later joined in business by the Tennant brothers. The premises moved in 1852 due to the expansion of the markets. A worker is pictured on the bottling line at the brewery in July 1962.

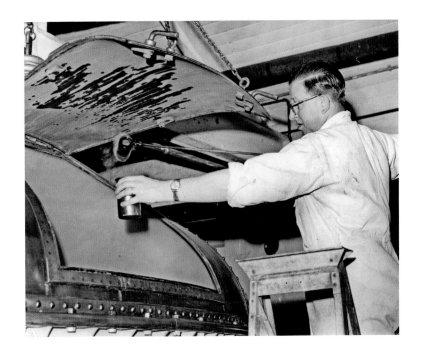

**Exchange Brewery, Bridge Street**

A worker checks the brew in July 1962. After the death of Edward Tennant in the early 1850s, the company was run by Robert Tennant and Thomas Moore, who later became the Lord Mayor of Sheffield between 1868 and 1871. Robert Tennant died in 1866 and was succeeded by his son, also called Robert. He was in charge until his own death in 1882.

**Exchange Brewery, Bridge Street**

Harry Gibson and John Elvin are seen weighing hops on 30 January 1963.

**Exchange Brewery, Bridge Street**

A scene in the Exchange Brewery lab on 6 July 1962. From the early 1850s, Tennant's Brewery sought to increase the amount of tied property it had in Sheffield. Over the years it steadily increased the number of pubs and off-licenses associated with them, even expanding into the area around Sheffield. Between 1916 and 1959 the company saw further expansion with the acquisition of a number of other brewerys from Sheffield and the surrounding area. 1961-1962 saw the merger of the company with Whitbread's Brewery of London, and the Exchange Brewery became responsible for the East Pennine area of the company. The Exchange Brewery closed in 1993.

**Fagan's, Broad Lane**

This picture of Fagan's was taken on 24 April 1995.

**Fagan's, Broad Lane**

Formerly titled the Barrel, the pub was renamed in 1985 to celebrate the achievement of Joe Fagan, the former landlord. He was Tetley's longest serving landlord, with thirty-seven years behind the bar. The pub has existed from at least the early 1820s, and past owners have included Thomas Rawson & Company Ltd. The above picture shows the change-over of the pub signs in 1985. Landlord Tom Boulding is pictured on the right.

**The Fairway, Birley Lane, Birley Wood**

The Fairway was a turn-off for the fairer sex, reported the *Star* of 5 July 1984. A beauty contest to be held by the pub had failed to attract any contestants, again. Manageress Gillian Harold told the paper: 'We just can't get girls to enter. We can't understand it. It's only a bit of fun with some nice prizes.' On offer for the winner was a photographic modelling session worth £150, flowers, cash and a place in the final for Miss Mansfield staged by Mansfield Inns.

**The Farfield Inn, Neepsend Lane**

Formerly belonging to the tied estates of brewers Greaves & Co., the premises have also been named Army Hotel, the Owl and Muff Inn. Their existence as a pub can be traced to the 1850s though the building is said to be much older. The photograph was taken on 17 April 1989. The premises gained Grade II listing status in December 1995, when the building was reported to date from 1753 with nineteenth- and mid-twentieth-century alterations.

**Far Lees, Leighton Road**

William Stones Ltd's latest pub was ready to open at the end of November 1963. The Far Lees was at the forefront of modern technology, equipped with underfloor electrical heating and electric pumps with beer meters. However, customers need not worry if there was a power cut and the pumps failed as a compressed air system was ready to spring into action. Customers were also free from a risk of frostbite as the heating system was to keep the pub at a constant temperature all the time, as opposed to the conventional radiator system. Another interesting feature was a conveyor system to transfer bottles of beer from the cellar to the bar at the push of a button. The new landlord was Fred Martin, previously of the Freedom Hotel, Walkley. Both pictures were taken on 20 November 1963.

**Fat Cat, Alma Street**

University economics lecturer David Wickett and his business partner, city solicitor Bruce Bentley, were at the forefront of the real ale trend in the early 1980s. They bought the former Alma pub in Alma Street at public auction for £33,750 in July 1981 and were to turn it into a pub with an emphasis on traditional ales and food. The pub was renamed the Fat Cat and since then has gone from strength to strength. William Stones' Cannon Brewery had brought the Alma into their tied estate in 1875.

**Ferret & Trouserleg, St James Street**

'I liked the service.' It probably wasn't the first time this description was used in the building occupied by the Ferret & Trouserleg. It had previously housed a school for choir boys and was one of the oldest church buildings in Sheffield. At the start of 1999 it had a different association as the Ferret & Trouserleg had just won a customer service award for the north of England. The pub beat 1,600 establishments to win the award from the Scottish and Newcastle Brewery. Licensee Mel Graveling was thrilled and said: 'I make sure we get staff with the right attitude and personalities so the customers receive a warm welcome.' Manager Toby Flint, Sarah Hunter and Gavin Peachey are pictured at the Ferret & Trouser Leg in October 1999.

**Fighting Cock, Montenay Crescent**

The landlord of the Fighting Cock was spitting feathers in February 1990 as the pub had been the victim of a third robbery in ten days. Thieves broke in through the back window and emptied a games machine of over £350. Landlord Noel Fletcher said: 'It is getting to be a ridiculous state of affairs here. The brewery won't pay for a burglar alarm, saying it is my responsibility even though it is their property being stolen.' Over £1,000 in cash along with drinks and cigarettes had been taken. The photograph was taken on 23 April 1962.

**Flares, West Street**

'It's brash it's garish and the punters love it,' shouted the *Star* on 14 August 1998, concluding that if any southerner were to accuse Sheffield of being stuck in a time warp they wouldn't be far wrong. A big part of the reason was Flares, a new themed city centre pub which had opened with an outrageous agenda: to celebrate the '70s in all its platform-booted, kipper-tied glory. The retro epidemic had spread to the newly renovated West Street Hotel where the dress code was definitely strict – strictly bad! Pictured outside Flares pub are (from left to right): Ali Baker, Rachel Watson, Ben Marshall (Huggy Ben) and Ken Odoki-Olam.

## Fleur de Lys, Totley Hall Lane

The *Star* of 29 January 1960 reported that landlord Roy Watson had installed a reaction meter in the Fleur de Lys, Totley. The aim of the device was to remind customers who were driving of the effect that drink had on their reactions. Roy said: 'If anyone doubts it [that reactions are slower after a drink], this machine will give proof. I've never known it to fail yet ... Often a customer will check his reactions as soon as he comes in and before leaving he will make a second check. He's always slower.' Formerly belonging to William Stones, the premises were rebuilt during the 1930s. The top picture was taken in *c.* 1920 when Tom Kirby was the landlord; the one below was taken on 15 January 1981.

**Floozy & Firkin, Chesterfield Road**

June 1996 saw the newest addition to the Firkin pub chain open in what used to be the Woodseats Hotel. The opening was aided by model Melanie Shepherd, who when posing outside proved quite a distraction for passing motorists. The pub was the second Firkin outlet in Sheffield, joining the Foundry & Firkin in West Street. The chain had ninety pubs across the country and were known for their irreverence and outrageous sense of humour. Four years later the pub reverted to its original title of Woodseats, but has since been converted into a curry house.

### Floozy & Firkin, Chesterfield Road

The *Sheffield Star* of 14 November 1996 reported that the name of one of the drinks at the Floozy & Firkin had caused offence to female customers and was to be changed. Male customers saw the funny side when ordering a pint of 'Slapper', but after complaints it was renamed Can-Can. A spokeswoman for the Firkin chain said: 'The pub itself is light hearted, the whole Firkin thing is intended to be off-the-wall and a bit quirky. The names of the beers, slogan and the memorabilia all reflect that. Slapper was meant in that spirit, but obviously it has been taken a little bit too seriously and customers lodged complaints. We listened and said "change it".' However, customers could still order a pint of 'Missionary' or a jug of 'Floozy'.

### The Forest Hotel, Rutland Road

In September 1985 the Forest Hotel (traceable to at least 1871) was to become the last 'beer only' pub in Sheffield. This was because the other, the Staffordshire Arms in Sorby Street, was about to be granted a spirits licence. Landlady Phyllis Pryor was not worried by her pub's status and she said: 'We do most of our trade during the afternoons when factory workers pop in after a shift and they aren't interested in spirits at that time.' After Phyllis retired in 1989, the Forest underwent a £100,000 refurbishment and finally received a spirits licence in 1990.

### Foresters Inn, Rockingham Street

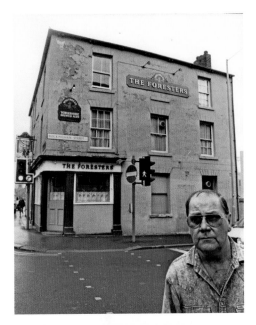

Landlord Anthony Baines is pictured outside the Foresters Inn, on the corner of Rockingham Street and Division Street, on 27 October 1988. It was reported by the *Star* on 16 March 1983 that he was 'shell-shocked' after a vault containing oyster shells was discovered while builders were digging footings for a new extension. This mystifying discovery was explained by a *Star* reader who informed that an oyster dealer had premises next to the pub in 1903 and had probably dumped the shells in the vault.

### Foresters Inn, Division Street/Rockingham Street corner

When the pub re-opened after refurbishment on 3 January 1990, Lord Mayor Tony Damms was called in to do the honours. Watching on (from left to right) are: Robbie Halkett Whitbread tenanted director, and tenants Peter and Barbara Moffatt. The premises, extending back to at least 1828 have also been titled Yorick, The Yorl and Olive Bar. As the Foresters Inn it was formerly tied to Shepherd, Green & Hatfield's Neepsend Brewery and subsequently absorbed into the Strouts & Waterman Brewery estate.

**Freemasons Arms, Walkley Lane**
Landlord Graham Pugh was back in Hillsborough in 1987 to take the reins of the Freemasons Arms (extending back to at least 1825 and formerly belonging to the tied estate of J. L. Cockayne & Sons). Graham had started his first career just a stone's throw away from the pub, playing in midfield for Sheffield Wednesday between 1965 and 1972, making 142 league appearances. He also played for Huddersfield Town, Chester City, Barnsley and Scunthorpe United. He is pictured with wife Susan outside the pub in May 1996. The bottom picture was taken *c*. 1936 when H. E. Tindall was the licensee.

*Above left:* **Frog & Parrot, Division Street**

Upon its opening in April 1982, new landlord Gary Campion (pictured left) of the Frog & Parrot, formerly the Prince of Wales, could boast two things: he was probably the only landlord in Sheffield brewing his own beer, and the decor was intentionally reminiscent of the 1940s. Two bitters were being brewed on the premises and at the time it was being produced at a rate of four barrels a day. The stronger of the two was called 'Reckless' but the other was as yet unnamed and a competition was to be held to find the best name, with first prize being a gallon of real ale. Of the decor Gary said: 'We have totally rejected the plastic approach of pubs nowadays. We want to create a '40s-type atmosphere – with the help of our customers.' Entertainment was provided in the form of a piano with a '40s pub pianist.

*Above right:* **Frog & Parrot, Division Street**

Roger Nowill (pictured right) later became landlord and embraced and expanded the brewing done on the premises. By the late 1980s, Roger had five ales being brewed in the Frog and Parrot with the most notable being 'Roger and Out'. The beer, introduced in July 1985, was claimed by Roger to be the strongest beer in the world, with a gravity of 1125. To protect his customers, the beer was served in glasses holding only a third of a pint, and customers were limited to three glasses a day. Drinkers would also receive a certificate with the first third, a yellow card for the second, before being given a red card and cut-off. In June 1988 the beer was recognised as the strongest regularly pulled beer in the world by the Guinness Book of World Records. Roger said: 'We've had enthusiasts who have come from as far as Paraguay, Moscow, Iran, Canada and Australia to try it.'

**Fulwood Inn, Tapton Park Road**
The Fulwood Inn opened in May 1999 after a million-pound refurbishment saw it transformed from a derelict steel baron's home into a pub and restaurant. The restoration saw the retention of original features, adding to the high-class decoration chosen by owners Mansfield Brewery. However, many local residents might not have been pleased to have this new addition to Ranmoor as they had waged a three-year war to try and stop planning permission. Further complaints arose after the Fulwood Inn was declared a child-free zone. The brewery allegedly said that it was an adult themed pub and the people they were aiming to attract didn't want their meal spoilt by children running around. The first managers of the pub were Linda and Gerald Jones, pictured.

**Gate, Attercliffe Common**

Exterior view of the (Old) Gate Inn, *c.* 1988. The premises were demolished shortly afterwards.

**Gate, Attercliffe Common**
Interior view of the (Old) Gate Inn, *c.* 1988.

**Gate Inn, Wadsley Bridge**
 The Gate Inn, Wadsley Bridge, was said by the *Sheffield Telegraph* of 13 June 1963 to have won its place on the culinary map after £2,000 worth of alterations. Landlord Charles Parkin had spent the money converting an old reception room at the pub into one of the most up-to-date dining rooms in Sheffield. The reason for this work was that a lot of top-flight business executives were based in the area and needed an upmarket place to visit for their lunch. The restaurant had space for fifty seats and was fitted with modern furnishings including a £400 carpet.

### Gate Inn, Wadsley Bridge

In December 1973, regulars of the of the Gate failed with a petition to keep the pub open at least until a replacement could be built behind it. Sheffield Corporation was to clear the pub for a road improvement scheme and rejected the plea. The premises could be traced back to at least 1822. The new pub opened in August 1975 with a novel feature introduced to curb football hooliganism. Four small spot lamps were installed that would flood the pub with light as soon as violence flared. The measure was suggested by a Bass Charrington architect who had some success with the feature in Birmingham. It must have been out of action when fifty brawling customers wrecked the pub at last orders in July 1991. The picture was taken on 28 June 1980.

### Gladstones, St James Street

Early in December 1987 Grand Metropolitan were battling to open their Sheffield venture when Magistrates refused their application for a drinks licence. Gladstones pub and restaurant was to be located in Church House, St James Street, which was a Grade II listed building and had already undergone £350,000 of refurbishment work. The bench said that the building was not suitable for a public house and that the proposed licensee was not a fit person to hold one. The city council and fire service had raised no objections to the building being used as a pub and the company was to appeal. On 19 December 1987 it was reported that the appeal was successful and a licence was granted. The picture was taken on 2 December 1987.

### The Grapes, Trippet Lane

It was with deep regret that, in February 1987, landlord Bob Rhodes called a halt to folk music nights that had taken place at the Grapes in Trippet Lane for almost twenty-five years. Bob was forced to stop the nights by a number of factors including rising rates and pressure from the brewery to make more money. The folk club and a number of others were being forced away because they used the room for free, which had been the case for years. Bob said: 'I'm having to turf them out because I have to make the room pay. It's that or my job, the brewery want me to make more out of the pub.' He added: 'I'm going to miss them all. They have been good to me all these years. I'm sorry to see them go.' A snooker table was moved into the room but the folk club, that had hosted acts such as Ralph McTell, Billy Connolly and Mike Harding at the pub, had returned by February 1992. The photograph dates from 29 March 1982.

### Great Britain Hotel, John Street

The Great Britain Hotel, pictured when it was tied to John Smith's Tadcaster Brewery and Athur Bullivant was the landlord. The premises were acquired by the Cockayne brothers in 1879.

**Grennell Mower, Low Edges Road, Greenhill**

In July 1957 a new pub was to open to serve the residents of the Greenhill-Bradway housing estate. The name chosen for the new pub, Grennell Mower, had a particular association with the area. In years gone by, the people of Greenhill were noted throughout South Yorkshire for the skill and speed of their mowing and also for the quality of the scythes produced in the village. The pub building had more modern aspirations with the interior and exterior design. It was built by Thorntons Ltd of Sheffield and designed by architect J. Foster of Duncan, Gilmore & Co. Ltd. The picture dates from 16 July 1957.

**Greyhound Inn, Attercliffe Road**

On 28 March 1991 it was reported that eighteen people were found by a policeman drinking after hours in the Greyhound Inn on Attercliffe Road. The landlord denied the charge of selling liquor outside permitted hours but was found guilty by magistrates and fined. The court was told that the landlord had admitted to the policeman that he had sold the drinks but told him: 'You cannot make ends meet if you don't sell after hours, it's the only way you can make a living.' After receiving a summons the landlord tried to change his story saying that it was a private party for a friend, but the magistrate said that if that was the case it would have been explained at the time.

**Greyhound Inn, Attercliffe Road**
The Greyhound formerly belonged to Thomas Marrian & Company Ltd's brewery and is pictured here on 15 October 1981.

**Half Moon, Mather Road**
Young patients at Sheffield's Children's Hospital were to have their own magazine in November 1982 thanks to regulars of the Half Moon. Some of the pub's energetic regulars raised £150 when they took part in the Sheffield Marathon, to buy a duplicator for the hospital. The photograph dates from 7 December 1960.

**Hallamshire House, Commonside, Walkley**
Joan Cardwell – barmaid at the Hallamshire
House for twenty-five years – pulls another pint
in December 1998.

**Hallamshire House, Commonside, Walkley**
Former Accrington Stanley player Les May at the Hallamshire House, Walkley.

### Harlequin, Johnson Street

At one time the inn was named Harlequin & Clown and two former landladies had a strong interest in music. The *Star* of 14 November 1980 said that landlady Joyce Gregg had made the pub into an Elvis Presley shrine. 'For the king of rock 'n' roll looks out from big colour posters and pictures around the walls ... You can expect to hear some of the golden Presley hits on her background cassette when the jukebox isn't playing,' said the newspaper. In December 2000, after more than ten years at the Harlequin, licensee Linda Greatorex was leaving, taking her music with her. Under Linda's control, the Harlequin became renowned as one of the best places in Sheffield to hear live folk and other acoustic music. She had even introduced an annual Bob Dylan festival and song-writing and literary competitions. Interestingly, on 19 June 1997, the pub staged Katie Sheldon's first 'Love in the Underworld' – an inventions and innovations evening. The pub's history extends back to at least 1822. The photograph on the right was taken on 20 November 1995.

## Hermitage, London Road

The old inn of the same name was destroyed during the blitz of December 1940. A new pub, designed by Hadfield, Cawkwell & Davidson, Sheffield, and built by A. Bradbury & Son (Contractors) Ltd, Sheffield, was opened in February 1963. The frontage of the building featured a 10-foot-high mural on ceramic tiles. The picture showed a hermit by the entrance of his cave home, surrounded by the herbs and foods on which he lived. The crowning glory of the interior was the balcony, reached by a curved staircase and overlooking the main room. The first host and hostess of the new premises were William Fisher and his wife Rita, who were formerly stewards at the Abbeydale Park Pavilion Club. In January 1984, strippers were a 'recent innovation' at the Hermitage by landlord, George Dalton. He had taken over the pub, his first, nearly five years earlier. 'While there are plenty of pubs in London Road, there's virtually no live entertainment so I've tried to build it up … I thought I'd experiment with strip and it has made a lot of difference. Takings have trebled, ' he said.

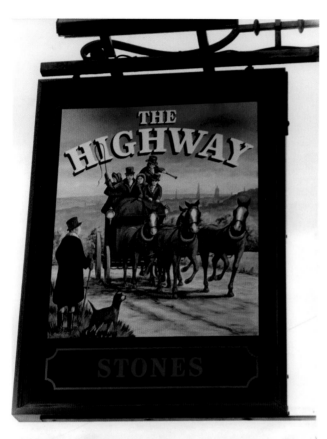

**Highway, Fox Street**

By January 1992, the Highway was celebrating four months as a free house and being run as a family partnership by landlord Bill Stead, son Paul and daughters Katherine and Selina. In May, Bill was to celebrate his fourth anniversary at the pub. Sadly, his wife Margaret died in 1990 but the family decided to carry on pulling pints. In 1995, 21-year-old Paul took over from his dad. He was one of the youngest landlords in the city. Charles Stead and son Paul are seen in the picture below on 7 July 1995.

**Highway, Fox Street**
The Highway pub is pictured on 4 March 1963.

**Hogshead, Orchard Square**
'Where the Hogshead dared to tread others followed,' claimed the *Star* on 28 September 1994. At that time it was among the first to revert back to traditional pub values and real ale and it arguably sparked a rash of copycats. It featured a choice of eight cask ales during the week and ten at weekends. There was even Barnsley Bitter brewed in Elsecar. The Hogshead was previously the Museum and the Orchard after that. The top picture taken in August 1999 shows Mark Simmonite of The Hogshead with a selection of ciders. Also pictured are, from left, Jane Hague, Alyson Jones and Kelsey James.

**Hogshead, Orchard Square**

The above photograph depicts Stuart Greener (centre seated) presenting Rebecca Linney (centre left) and Steve Roberts (centre right) and their team of staff with a team hospitality award in August 1997.

**Hope & Anchor Brewery, Mowbray Street**

Christopher Carter, Eleazor Milner and George Bird began brewing ales and stout under the title of Carter, Milner & Bird from Mowbray Street in 1892. Shortly afterwards it became the Hope Brewery and was incorporated as a public company in 1899. The picture here, inside the Hope & Anchor Brewery, was taken on 1 July 1961.

## Hope & Anchor Brewery, Mowbray Street

The early years of the twentieth century saw the brewery close for a time. Eleazor Milner and George Bird died and William Earnest Bird (George Bird's son) took on the floundering business. By 1938, following years of struggle, the company was housed in new premises in Clay Wheels Lane, Wadsley Bridge. In 1942 the Hope Brewery merged with the Anchor Brewery (of Henry Tomlinson) to become Hope & Anchor Breweries Ltd. Expansion of the business in 1946 saw the company acquire the interests of Wheatley & Bates in Napier Street. From the early 1950s, further breweries were acquired, including Truswells (Sheffield), Wilkinson's Pine Street Brewery (Newcastle), Dawson Bros (Newcastle), Bramley's (Liverpool), Welcome Brewery (Oldham) and Openshaw Brewery (Manchester). Both pictures were taken on 1 July 1961.

**Hope & Anchor Brewery, Mowbray Street**

By the early 1960s the Hope & Anchor tied estate numbered some 240 houses. The company was subsequently taken over by Charrington United Breweries being amalgamated later into Bass-Charrington. The picture shows bottles of Carling lager leaving the pasteurizer in the bottling store on 1 July 1961.

**Horse & Groom, Blackstock Road**

Before Wilfred Campbell, aged 58, and his 55-year-old wife Nellie took over the Horse & Groom, it had not been involved with charity work. But in July 1973, after just over a year and a half at the pub, the couple had organised dozens of efforts for charity and earned a prize from film star Richard Attenborough. The prize – an inscribed tankard – was for raising £162 in a national pub contest organised by the Muscular Dystrophy Group. The Horse and Groom came twenty-eighth out of 400 pubs.

**Horse & Groom, Blackstock Road**

The pub underwent a £140,000 transformation by July 1988, when Tetley's Brewery made it into an 'impact pub'. Gone were the traditional tap room and public bar in favour of one large lounge with a raised games area. Young licensees Fred and Andrea Fearn (pictured), who took on the Horse & Groom as their first pub in April 1988, were looking forward to seeing the looks of amazement on their customers' faces when they stepped through the new entrance door. David Craggs of Phoenix Architecture and Interiors, formerly chief architect for the brewery, was responsible for the pub's new interior design. The above photograph dates from 19 July 1988.

**Horse & Jockey Chesterfield Road**

The photograph was taken in *c*. 1925 when John Jordan was the landlord and the house was tied to Tennants.

**Hodson Hotel, Carlisle Road**

The Hodson Hotel was photographed on 13 October 1967 when tied to John Smith's. The premises closed in 1970.

### The Howard Hotel, Howard Street

In December 1990 the Howard Hotel was looking to bury its sometimes dubious past and look to the future with new found confidence. A £250,000 Mansfield Brewery investment saw the rundown brewers' Tudor-style premises transformed. Hotel was being dropped from the name and ready to take over were Gary and Karen Dunn who, after spells in Wakefield and Harrogate, spent four months at the Surrey, while waiting for the Howard to take shape. A Hallam FM broadcast with giveaways helped to put the Howard back on the map, but eyebrows were raised when a quiz, hosted by DJ Dave Kilner, was won by a scratch team from the pub itself! The Howard is one of several pubs in the Sheffield area using the family name of the Dukes of Norfolk. The Howard Hotel (bottom right) is seen here from Parkhill on 19 June 1965 before the surrounding area was redeveloped.

**The Industry Inn, Main Road, Darnall**
Peter and Marilyn Flynn are pictured outside Ward's Industry Inn on 2 November 1984. The premises were acquired by S.H. Ward & Company in 1873.

**The Jack-in-a-Box, Silkstone Road, Hackenthorpe**
The first pint of beer at the Jack-in-a-Box was pulled in 1968 by Sheffield brewery chief, W. A. Wright. 'The new pub in Silkstone Road will cater for the City Council's new estate now being built,' said Mr Wright, chairman and managing director of S. H. Ward & Company Ltd, Sheaf Brewery, at the informal opening ceremony. Believed to be the only pub in the North with the name Jack-in-a- Box, it boasted two ground floor bars and first-floor accommodation for the new tenants, David Wood and his wife Joyce. Twenty-two years later the pub underwent a major refurbishment when it was part of the managed house division of the Vaux Group, but it was still to be supplied by S. H.Ward Ltd and stock all of Ward's popular brands. Pub managers George and June Gillott were very proud of the house, having been resident on the estate for many years before entering the licensed trade.

### John O' Gaunt, Blackstock Road

The John O'Gaunt featured a number of times in the news in the 1990s. First there was a fifty-strong police drugs raid on the premises in March 1992. A 16-year-old school leaver was cautioned and another customer bailed after a police operation which lost the landlord £500 in takings from a rave night at the pub. He was reported as saying: 'It doesn't surprise me that this is all fifty coppers have managed. It was a farce.' Around 1995 the pub got a boost when it was chosen to feature in the Pint O' Bitter film starring Sean Bean. 'The location manager thought it was marvellous and the producer and directors fell in love with it. I think they looked at about 40 or 50 pubs before choosing us,' said landlady Gloria Eastwood. In June 1996 Brendan Dignam was stabbed at the John O'Gaunt. Landlord Sean McNally, 38, said: 'I could not believe it ... Two men left the pub and moments later everything went berserk, with seven police cars turning up with flashing lights. Then I realised something serious had gone off.' Brendan Dignam was reported at the time to be ill but stable in hospital.

### John O' Gaunt, Blackstock Road
The pub is pictured boarded up on 26 August 2002.

## Jolly Buffer, Ecclesall Road

Jolly Buffer pub landlady Debbie Harvey could have done with just that when she parachuted for charity in July 1988. The landing was far from soft when plucky Debbie took the plunge with regulars from the pub – she broke her leg in two places. Others in the nine-strong group were nursing a few bruises after the mass parachute jump. One landed in a bush and another in a tree. Landlord Terry said: 'I was supposed to be doing the jump too but my boss said only one of us should do it in case we had an accident and this has proved to be right.' Despite the calamities the stunt raised over £800 for Sheffield's Jessop Hospital special baby care unit. A year later the pub went from being managed to tenanted by Paulene and Mike Gent who had spent the previous eighteen months at the Swan Inn, Main Road, Ridgeway. There, the couple established a reputation for live Country music and that was to continue at the Jolly Buffer. Incredibly, when Mike hacked down bushes on the patio he uncovered a wall carving of a cutlery worker. Later, on 7 November 1989, a special event was to be staged marking the tenth anniversary of a pub that was opened by the then Mistress Cutler as a £175,000 homage to a proud Sheffield tradition. The top picture was taken on 22 February 1980; the bottom one on 21 September 1995.

### King's Head, Manchester Road

In February 1958 it was stated that the modernisation of the King's Head, Crosspool, was one more in the campaign by Tennant Bros Ltd to make the local something more than just a building for the sale of liquor. The brewery wanted every one of its 500 houses to be a place worth visiting with everything to order in the way of comfort and entertainment. Tennants had boasted their own building department for many years and in 1946, they appointed M. W. Ofield as their own architect. Since then, Ofield and his department had designed three new public houses and were responsible for all types of structural alterations to scores of others. The King's Head was about the eightieth house in which the brewery had carried out major structural modernisation and alterations in post-war years. When the brewery took over the King's Head in the 1880s it was a solid built country local. Its main assets were a bowling green and a store for the bowls. In 1910 the brewery altered the building adding a billiard room, bathroom and kitchen. The cellar was also enlarged. The changes in 1958 were more sweeping. The comfort of the landlord and his family and that of the customers received equal consideration. The landlord at that time was A. V. Walsh.

**King's Head, Manchester Road**

On 27 November 1985 the King's Head was boasting another new look. The premises had been closed for three weeks and the property had been extended and transformed. A right royal nosh up was available as the pub had been turned into a Beefeater Steakhouse. Beefeater houses were owned by Whitbread but operated as a separate company. The new pub got its official kick off courtesy of Sheffield Wednesday stars Gary Shelton and Brian Marwood at a special opening ceremony with invited guests on 26 November. Consequently, nobody at that time would have guessed the pub would be demolished fifteen years later. On 29 September 2000 it was reported that the saga of the King's Head had rolled to an end. Councillors reluctantly decided to allow developers to build thirty-two flats for the over-50s on the site of the former pub. Their officers said there were no planning grounds for refusal. But councillors made clear their anger over the way the old pub, a landmark in Crosspool, had been demolished so quickly, albeit legally, in the face of widespread public opposition. At one point, local protesters had staged a week-long sit-in at the pub in an effort to save it from demolition.

**King's Head, Manchester Road**
King's Head protest in March 2000. Barry Everard (right) with some of the protesters outside of the former pub on Manchester Road.

84

## Little Mesters, Broomhall

In March 1979 the Little Mesters at the junction of Broomhall and William Street was Mansfield Brewery's new public house in Sheffield, on one of the smallest sites developed by the brewery. The total area for the building was only a little over 400 square metres, which brought about building difficulties as all materials had to be stored away from the area. Around the walls were old photographs and prints depicting Sheffield when the cutlery industry was in its heyday, at least in terms of the number of 'Little Mesters' or out-workers supplying their skills to the larger established companies. Five years later, in September 1984, controversy hit the pub when time was called on the landlord. He had previously been sent on a two-week holiday by Mansfield Brewery to 'rethink' the resignation he had tendered. But in the interim, Mansfield accepted his resignation and were ready to appoint a new landlord. The controversy began a month earlier when he was accused by Broomhall Community Group of failing to prevent racist abuse and attacks at the Little Mesters. It called for his removal but Mansfield insisted they had faith in him. The dispute led to angry meetings between brewery officials and local residents and pickets were mounted outside the pub on two weekends. Mansfield Brewery general manager Terry Boddington said: 'After long discussions with the landlord and his wife we have decided to accept their resignation ... We are now looking for someone to fill the vacancy and restore the stability the Little Mesters requires.

### Little Mesters, Broomhall

In August 1989 there was confusion regarding the Little Mesters' future, prompting the licensees, Ann and Dave Hardy, to issue a message – it really is business as usual. But some drinkers confused a campaign to save the area's historic little mesters' workshops with the future of the pub itself. So, the couple, who had been at the pub for only a few months, were keen to point out the pub was definitely not due for demolition. 'One lady even said she was going to get a petition up to keep us open,' said Ann. 'We have only just arrived and we have no intention of going anywhere yet.' The top picture was taken on 5 January 1981; the one below of Ann and Dave Hardy was taken on 26 August 1989.

**Manchester Hotel, Nursery Street**

Despite the changes which were made over a six-week period in 1990, it was said that the Manchester Hotel (it has also been known as the Manchester Railway Hotel and Manchester & Lincolnshire Railway Hotel) retained its familiar friendly atmosphere. 'It was homely even though it was a bit shabby. It was a man's pub. We had just a few lunch time customers, they were workers for their lunchtime pints and sandwiches. The brewery has altered it without kicking the guts out of it,' said Lynda Turner who ran the pub with husband Bob. A garage at the back was demolished and a new games room meant extra room could be found to enlarge the bar area. Also adding to the new facilities was a kitchen in the old pool room. Lynda and Bob are pictured here on 30 November 1990.

**Manchester Hotel, Nursery Street**

Interior of pub after refurbishment, 26 November 1990. In *A Complete History of The Great Flood at Sheffield* Samuel Harrison states that on 11 and 12 March 1864, 'The Manchester Railway Hotel had its entire front broken down.' The premises became part of the William Bradley Soho Brewery tied estate in 1870.

**Milton Arms, Thomas Street/Milton Lane corner**

A group of regulars pose outside the Milton Arms before a trip to the races, *c.* 1924. The premises existed between 1825 and 1964.

**Manor Hotel, Fretson Road**

Manor Hotel landlord Paddy Maloney is pictured with customers on 27 July 1989. On 23 December 1992 the *Star* informed that the Manor Hotel had been transformed into the new Fairleigh Social Club. A special evening of entertainment was laid on for members of the social club, which had been without a home for nearly two years after leaving an annexe at nearby St Theresa's church. The club bought the pub from former owners Bass when it had to slash its number of premises to comply with new restrictions on monopolies. The building had been badly vandalised and hit by two fires in the years it lay empty. It took builder David Ford eight weeks to renovate it.

**Manor Castle Inn, Edward Street, Netherthorpe**

The premises can be traced to the mid-nineteenth century and are seen here when tied to Truswells', and when G. Marshall was the licensee. The picture dates from *c.* 1930.

**Marples Hotel, Fitzalan Square**

At 11.44 p.m. on Thursday 12 December 1940, a German high explosive bomb scored a direct hit on the Marples Hotel. Shortly before that, customers and staff were singing to the accompaniment of gunfire. About seventy people died in the wreckage but seven were rescued alive. It was the worst single tragedy of that terrible night. 'For years we put a wreath on the site and so did other people,' said a spokesman for John Smith's Tadcaster Brewery Company Ltd. He was speaking on 5 February 1957 after plans were approved for a new Marples Hotel at Sheffield Brewster Sessions. These were drawn by Sir Bertram Wilson, chartered architect and surveyor to the brewery. On the evening of 30 April 1959 the new Marples Hotel stood tall, white and majestic at the High Street/Fitzalan Square corner and opened its doors for the first time. But it was predicted that it would not be a 'normal' first night as the palatial and modern new hotel was practically built on the pyre of the original. The top picture shows people being rescued from the Marples in December 1940 and the one below shows the Marples' ruins on 16 October 1956.

## Marples Hotel, Fitzalan Square

The seventy dead from 1940 were remembered on a bronze plaque that was unveiled by the Lord Mayor of Sheffield, Alderman John W. Holland. The plaque was just inside the High Street entrance to the hotel. The building itself was a simple steel-framed structure, clad externally in Portland stone and small amounts of marble. Remarkably, it was the first time that Sheffield officially had a Marples Hotel. The licence for the new premises was granted in that name. The 'old' Marples was only so called by popular consent. It appeared in the records as 'Market Street Wine Vaults'. In 1881 its owner was John Marples and the licensee Edward Marples, and it was from that time that it became popularly known as Marples. The top picture shows an exterior view taken on 29 April 1959. The picture below of the bar was taken at the same time.

**Marples Hotel, Fitzalan Square**

On 17 December 1974 the Marples re-opened after an £80,000 facelift. This included an entertainment lounge incorporated on the ground floor and downstairs was a bar and discotheque with a late-night licence. It was to be re-opened by ex-Alderman Jim Stirland who had been chairman of the council's planning committee when the pub was first rebuilt. In 1989, the Marples closed once again for an extensive refurbishment that lasted three months, reopening on 25 May. Wayne Chadwick, operations director of Mine Host Inns, which was operating the pub for John Smith's, was to become the new manager until a permanent replacement could be found. The new Marples was aiming to go upmarket, with its ground-floor lounge, marble-clad pillars, spotlights, neon strips and video monitors installed in the lower bar area downstairs. The top picture, dating from 20 July 1990, shows Bert Malkin who had been drinking at the Marples for sixty years. The picture below taken on 23 May 1989 shows a group of staff (from left): Wayne Chadwick, general manager; Bill and Sue Morrison, managers; and Graham Robinson, tenanted sales manager for John Smith's.

**Milestone, Crystal Peaks, Waterthorpe**

Yorkshire County Cricket skipper Phil Carrick bowled along to run his first pub in December 1988. Wolverhampton and Dudley Breweries selected the all-rounder because the Milestone was the company's first outlet in Yorkshire which, in Black Country eyes, was synonymous with cricket. Having had a quick rehearsal, he pulled the first pint of the famed Banks's, raised his glass and noting a uniform among the assembled guests, stressed, 'I'm not driving, sir.' The response was immediate, 'And, I'm not a policeman, sir,' said the fire officer. Managers David and Angela Fisher (pictured) were first hosts of Wards' Hawk & Dove, which could just be glimpsed from the Milestone. That was in 1981 and the Fishers stayed for five-and-a-half years, having previously been at the Domino, Eggerton Street, the Three Feathers Inn, Prince of Wales Road and a Ferrybridge hostelry. After their first Waterthorpe residency they strayed to Tetley's Golden Fleece, Chesterfield, but Angela, a former licensed ladies president, was keen to return to the area. During 1989 the couple scooped two pub awards.

**Milestone, Crystal Peaks, Waterthorpe**
Exterior view of Milestone on 11 October 2009. Reproduced courtesy of John Law.

**Mulberry Tavern, Mulberry Street**

Proposed alterations to the alleged 229-year-old Mulberry Tavern were approved at Sheffield Transfer Sessions on 6 July 1954, though W. Scholey, presiding, said the place would lose some of its old character. 'But the changes will be advantageous to the public,' he added. W. B. Siddons, for John Richdale & Co. Ltd, said the Tavern was one of Sheffield's oldest inns. The date of the building was about 1725. It was planned to reconstruct the whole of the ground floor to provide a lounge, bar-lounge and a small 'snug' with a central servery. At that time there were four public rooms. Harry Armitage, architect of Surrey Street, was responsible for the interior design. A theory about how the pub acquired its name has been put forward. King James I decreed that Mulberry trees be planted wherever possible to help produce silk. At that time the gardens between High Street and Norfolk Street were eminently suitable and the King's command was obeyed. The pub was in that area. The picture on the left was taken on 3 September 1968; the one on the right was taken on Thursday 8 March 1973 before Saturday closure.

**Mulberry Tavern, Mulberry Street**

The Tavern – as all good taverns should – had a mystery associated with it. Once, when a commercial traveller booked in for the night, he was found dead the next morning in the cellar. It was assumed he had fallen through a trap door. Curiously, he had no identification on him, although a large sum of money was in his possession. No one came forward to identify him and he was buried in the parish churchyard. The Mulberry Tavern closed its doors for the last time on Saturday 10 March 1973 and was demolished. But out of the rubble, like a Phoenix rising from the ashes, a new Mulberry Tavern was opened nearby in Arundel Gate on 16 November 1976 by comedienne Marti Caine. The photograph on the left dates from 20 September 1973.

### Nailmaker's Arms, Blackmoor Road, Norton

Following a £50,000 refit at the Nailmaker's in August 1984, champion nail bender Ben Read visited the pub to join in with the re-opening celebrations. Ben, aged 51, from Hampshire, bent six-inch nails for charity. He claimed they were the most difficult size, but he could manage 100 every 13½ minutes. The former blacksmith challenged customers 50p a nail to match him. And landlady Pat Williams welcomed them back to the pub after a six-week break. 'This is a traditional English pub where the nailmakers from the cottages used to drink,' she said. Pictured at the re-opening ceremony, champion nail bender Ben Read demonstrates the art to William Younger's Inns Director John Campbell, left, and licensees Duggie and Pat Williams.

### Nailmaker's Arms, Norton

Applying for a publican's licence for the Nailmaker's Arms at Backmoor Road, a solicitor said at the Sheffield Transfer Sessions on 13 May 1958 that the origins of the premises 'were lost in the mists of antiquity'. Mr J. J. Mcavoy for the owner and licensee John Risker said the house was at present a beer house. It had been renovated in accordance with plans agreed about eighteen months earlier. Mr Risker told the bench that when he took over in 1954-55 he was selling an average of 2.35 barrels a week. During the previous year the average was 9.08 barrels. Every day he was being asked for spirits. The application was granted. The picture dates from 25 November 1957.

**Nelson Hotel, Furnival Gate**

On 8 April 1968 a man was stabbed in a bar of the Nelson Hotel in Furnival Gate, off the Moor. Joe Hancock of Albert Road, Heeley, was taken to Sheffield Royal Hospital, but died an hour after the attack. Customers said that the incident appeared to start as an argument in the lower bar of the hotel near the steps leading up to the street. Ian Stevenson was one of a group of five men who entered the hotel immediately after the attack. He said a youth rushed through the group just as they began to descend. The youth disappeared into the street. 'Then I heard someone scream from below, "Get me an ambulance, get me an ambulance." I rushed down and saw a fellow aged about 20 writhing on the floor. He was bleeding badly.' Mr Stevenson said the man was stabbed a number of times around the neck. He lifted the man up and tried to staunch his wounds. A girl came to his aid and together they managed to stop most of the bleeding until the ambulance arrived. Mr Stevenson said the man was moaning and only semi-conscious. The lower part of the hotel was believed to have been about half full at the time of the attack. A man was later charged with murdering Joseph Hancock. The picture dates from 18 October 1962.

**Norfolk Arms, Ringinglow Road**

Frans Hals' Laughing Cavalier, sometimes associated with the sound of things going bump in the night, was smiling happily down from the wall of the snug at the Norfolk Arms at Ringinglow in September 1988. But no one had been laughing in the pub while the William Stones' design team had gingerly set about recapturing the former interior of the seventeenth-century listed hostelry. Over the years the picture was said to have governed the movements of their resident ghost Eric, in raincoat and hat, who had been seen roaming through the rooms of the pub. It seems that years ago the Cavalier was removed from the wall at the suggestion of a former regular and a spate of bad luck promptly struck the pub. It ceased only when the painting was re-hung. Landlady Gill Murphy took it all very seriously: 'Eric has been seen by various no-nonsense type people who you would not have thought believed such things,' she commented, 'obviously whilst we have the Cavalier in residence on his wall, we have a happy pub.' In an effort to keep him happy, Stones' designer Dene Linley removed the mocking figure briefly and reframed him. 'He must have approved because nothing's happened yet, but it was a bit nerve-wracking,' added Gill. The picture above was taken on 16 March 1981.

**Nursery Tavern, Ecclesall Road**

In February 1986, Sheffield's oldest pub landlady, Vera Jenkins, who celebrated her 82nd birthday by sticking to her normal pint pulling routine, announced her retirement. This brought to an end more than half a century's link with the Nursery Tavern, Ecclesall Road. Although she wasn't actually born behind the bar, her service began when her father, Fred Hurst, was licensee. Vera learned the trade from him and apart from a spell at the old South Sea Hotel, Broomhill, kept up the tradition when her husband, George, was Nursery tenant. She took over when he died twenty years earlier and, with mainly female help, had run it on her own since then, maintaining the pub's tradition for hot, juicy pork sandwiches, which her father always thought would be a winner. When she was 80, Stones Brewery and regulars combined to lay on a spread. On her 82nd birthday, long-serving bar staff joined in to help her cut a birthday cake. The top picture was taken on 20 February 1984, and the one below on 27 February 1986.

## Office, Upperthorpe

In November 1991 it was reported that business had been brisk at The Office since the former Shipstone's house was revamped to provide and Upperthorpe haven for nearby Norwich Union workers and local residents. Inevitably, the new Upperthorpe Road free house, with its tongue-in-cheek name, aroused curiosity after standing idle for about fourteen months from closing as the Eversley House, but mine hosts Tony and Sue Smith (pictured here on 21 March 1996) were happy to report that most of the visitors had returned on a regular basis. During March 1996, thirsty Office regulars were plunged into darkness without a pint to sup after the pub was plagued by a spate of power cuts – twelve in two weeks to be precise. And this hit trade because the beer pumps wouldn't work, leaving staff unable to pull pints. One lasted from 7.20 p.m. on a Sunday night until five minutes before closing time at 10.30 p.m. Fed-up landlord Tony Smith groaned: 'As can be appreciated, all the customers had gone home. It cost us an arm and a leg.' In time, Yorkshire Electricity solved the problem.

## Old Bowling Green, Upwell Lane

The Old Bowling Green Hotel is pictured here on 11 December 1959, with Roy Ward as the licensee under a Tetley's tenancy. The sign to the left of the door reads: 'RAOB King Edward Lodge'. The premises were acquired by Thomas Marrian & Co. Ltd in 1895 and later came under Duncan Gilmour & Co. Ltd.

**Old Queen's Head, Pond Hill**

In July 1985 it was revealed that Audrey Garrett (pictured left), cleaner at the Old Queen's Head, shouted 'Good Morning!' before she went into the Snug. That was her way of telling anyone there that they'd better get out before she went in with duster, polish and vacuum cleaner. It did the trick. Audrey cleaned the Snug. She had adopted this routine since starting work at the pub three years earlier. Audrey was just one in a long line of cleaners who had been terrified of the Snug – an eerie little room with an ancient fireplace. In 1980 the manager was Roy Couldwell. One evening, Roy saw a little old man in the Snug with a pint of beer in his hand. A cleaner called Mary is said to have seen an elderly chap with two jugs in his hands, standing by the fireplace. The pub manager in Audrey Garrett's time was Joe Butler and he lived there with his two cats. They refused to go anywhere near the Snug. 'I try not to think about it too much,' he said. 'So often I feel as though something has passed me and I shiver. Everyone feels the presence of someone else and we can't pinpoint exactly what's going on. The photograph on the right was taken on 5 May 1966.

**Old Queen's Head, Pond Hill**

The timber-framed pub building is thought to date from *c.* 1475, although the earliest known written record of it is in an inventory compiled in 1582 when it was called 'The hawle at the Poandes'. By the beginning of the nineteenth century, the building was being used as a residence. In 1840 a pub called the Old Queen's Head was opened in the neighbouring building, and sometime after 1862 the pub expanded into this building. The premises were formerly tied to Thomas Berry's Brewery and later to Truswell's Brewery. The pub was given Grade II listed status in 1952 and was refurbished in 1993 to the tune of £750,000 as part of the Tom Cobleigh chain. The Queen in the pub's name is likely Mary, Queen of Scots, who was imprisoned in Sheffield from 1570 to 1584. The picture dates from 5 May 1966.

**Pheasant, Broad Street**

The Pheasant, looking towards Dixon Lane, *c.* 1905, when George Ward was the licensee. Dating from at least 1797, the pub became part of the Burton Weir Brewery tied estate in 1875 and closed in 1911.

### Plumpers, Bawtry Road, Tinsley

William Stones' Brewery announced in April 1965 that they were to demolish the Plumpers Hotel (dating from at least 1825) and rebuild it less than 20 yards away. It was in the way of a fly-over for the Sheffield and Leeds motorway. It was intended to build the new one before the demolition of the old. The new Plumpers had been in existence for approximately thirty-five years when licensee Wendy Fowler broke the news to her regulars that the pub was going to close. She said the brewery had given her only a short time to quit the pub so work could start to convert the premises into an American golf shop. Consequently, angry regulars launched a petition and planned to obstruct any development by handcuffing themselves to the pub. A spokesman for Punch Taverns who owned the premises, said: 'Plumpers has been run on a short term basis with temporary managers for the last five years. It's now time to develop the site.' On Tuesday night 11 April 2000 Plumpers closed without incident. The old Plumpers is pictured above on 3 September 1962, and the new one, below, is pictured on 16 November 1965.

**Pomona, Ecclesall Road**

A new pub opened in Sheffield's Eccelsall Road on 5 August 1980 but the celebrations were tinged with sadness. The new Pomona Hotel stood within sight and sound of its predecessor, a popular pub dating back to at least 1845 which was due to be bulldozed in the final phase of a development scheme. Last orders were called at the old Pomona on Sunday 3 August when the pub – a former vicarage – was packed with regulars calling to say farewell in a wake of black pudding and pork pies. The new pub was to be run by Brian Nichols and his wife Carol. 'It's smashing here,' said Brian. 'I can stand up in the cellar, I was bent double in the old one.' Home Brewery, who owned the Pomona were not amused to receive a compulsory purchase order from Sheffield City Council in July 1972, especially as their new pub had cost in the region of £200,000. The top picture dates from 1 April 1976 and the one below was taken on 15 June 1994.

### Porter Cottage, Sharrow Vale Road

In March 1996 the Porter Cottage (traceable to at least 1838 and tied to the Thomas Rawson Pond Street Brewery from 1855) was sporting a new inn sign. It was a dead ringer for the famous Edvard Munch painting 'The Scream'. But what was wrong with the old one? 'It was just four yokels and a leg of mutton sitting around a table in a tavern. Nobody can remember it already,' said landlord Tim Price. After a pub refurbishment he was thinking of ideas for a new sign when he saw a print of the famous Norwegian painting in an art shop. 'I am amazed I got away with it but it's been approved by a director. The Porter's loud, noisy – and it's a scream,' joked Tim. The bottom picture was taken by Dave Milner on 17 March 2000.

**Raven, Fitzwilliam Street**

In August 1980, it was reported that the inside of the Raven pub had been demolished and it was to be completely renovated in 'nautical' fashion, and the name was to be changed to 'Hornblower'. Workmen are seen undertaking repairs on the 8th of August. In subsequent years the pub was also known as O'Hagan's and Lounge. The pub dated back to at least 1833 and was formerly tied to A. H. Smith's Don Brewery. It has since been demolished.

**Real Macaw/Woodstock, Ecclesall Road**

In December 1996, customers ringing what they thought was the Real Macaw pub and diner on Ecclesall road were surprised to hear staff answer by saying Woodstock. The place had changed its name five times in the previous twelve years. Usually a new name arrived with a revamp but at that time it was for legal reasons, said general manager Peter Yates. 'There is another company which has registered the name Real Macaw. But a lot of regulars are pleased because they've always called it the Woodstock,' he explained. The premises were once titled the Prince of Wales and then became the Woodstock Diner. That changed to the Baltimore Diner but before long it became the Woodstock Exchange. The picture was taken on 11 August 1994.

**Rising Sun, Abbey Lane**

The pub's manager was hit over the head by a gunman and his wife and staff were tied up during a vicious robbery on 4 July 1993. Two thugs armed with revolvers burst into the pub after last orders. First they overpowered landlady Margaret Haywood and three members of the staff clearing up behind the bar. After tying them up with washing line, the men wearing balaclavas and gloves confronted John Haywood in his office. They squirted lemon juice into his eyes and hit him over the head with the gun. He was also tied up and the staff were told to lay on the floor while one of the robbers searched for the takings. Several thousand pounds, swelled by takings from a barbeque to celebrate American Independence Day, were seized. During October 1998 the Rising Sun closed for three months while over £300,000 was spent on extending the place. The pub can be traced to at least 1822 and was formerly tied to Henry Tomlinson's Anchor Brewery. The picture dates from 9 September 1955.

**Rising Sun, Abbey Lane**

The photograph shows the pub's new cocktail bar on 9 September 1955.

**Rising Sun, Jenkin Road, Brightside**

When former Sheffield Council employees, Terry and Sharon McNamara, took over the tenancy of the Rising Sun it was their first licensed trade venture. In July 1990, after two-and-a-half years in the job, Tetley honoured the pair with a tenancy award and Sheffield & District CAMRA followed that up with a pub of the month accolade. The Rising Sun's winning ways continued with top prize in the Tetley Exterior Pub Refurbishment of the Year Award scheme which had more than 100 entries. The couple are pictured here receiving the latter award on 30 July 1990 from the brewery's project and design surveyor, Tony Knapton.

**Rock House, Rock Street**

A tough landlord led the fight to rid the streets of drug pushers in August 1995. For a time the Rock House at Burngreave had a lurid reputation as a focal point for dealers in cocaine, heroin and cannabis. Police often mounted operations and raids at homes of locals. But ex-union official at Rock House, landlord Donnie McFarlane, aged 49, said there was a strengthening movement among ordinary folk to turn the tide against narcotics suppliers. Victory would mean handing the streets back for children to play in without the lurking presence of villains. Donnie's courageous stance won approval from police and churchmen. Sheffield City Council leader at that time, Mike Bower, who lived in the area for five years, added: 'It is evidence that people will eventually take some action to do something about what they regard as unacceptable social conditions in their area.'

### Rock, Dixon Lane

In November 1970, 68-year-old Sam Wilde was not looking forward to leaving the Rock pub in Dixon Lane after serving behind the bars there for nearly forty years. Members of the Wilde family had been pulling pints at the Rock for nearly a century. The tavern had been sold for about £30,000 to be turned into a shop because it was alleged Whitbread's (Yorkshire) Ltd considered that city centre pubs needed to be a bit more plush than the Rock and that conversion would be uneconomical. But Sam liked the pub as it was with its mahogany bars and tiny snug room, and not a juke box or one-armed-bandit in sight – although he had allowed a television set in one of the rooms. For the rest, the Rock was straight out of the 1890s. 'There aren't many of these places left, and the atmosphere's not the same in the modern pubs they're putting up these days,' said Sam. It was in the 1890s that Sam's mother Nellie went to work at the Rock for the Kirk family, who had held the licence since the 1830s. She started as a barmaid working long hours, and she and her husband William took over the place around 1901. Sam was born at the pub and he managed the place from 1921 until 1931, when he took over as licensee. In more recent years he had run it with the help of his daughter Margaret and her husband John. 'These walls could tell a few tales,' said Sam, and he talked about the time it was used by Belgian refugees during the First World War and the roaring '20s when country people would make a trip into Sheffield on Saturday – the husband to the football match and his wife to the shops – and both end up singing the night away in the Rock. The premises are said to date from the late eighteenth century and were once tied to A. H. Smith's Don Brewery (and later to Tennant Bros). The Rock closed in 1972.

**Rotherham House, Exchange Street**

Berni Inns, the Bristol-based catering chain, established by Welsh-Italian brothers Frank and Aldo Berni, announced they had acquired on lease the Rotherham House and the old No. 12 restaurant in the same building during September 1965. Both were owned by Tennant Brothers Ltd. The Rotherham House was formerly tied to Thos Berry & Co. Ltd. The takeover was one of seven announced at the same time, most of them involving inns in northern towns. Included was the Red Lion in Doncaster. The Rotherham House-Old No. 12 was the second Berni Inn in Sheffield. The first, the Norton at Meadowhead – also leased from Tennants – was opened in November of the previous year. A brewery spokesman said: 'They take over on November 1, but it will be some months before they open as a Berni because of extensive alterations.' It was planned to convert the premises in the same manner as the Norton, to a speciality restaurant that would continue to sell Tennants' products. The latest acquisitions were part of Berni's £5 million expansion programme and came just ten days after the announcement of record group profits of £1,410,000. The Berni chain was sold to Grand Metropolitan in 1970 and then to Whitbread in 1995.

**Royal George, Carver Street**

The Royal George, situated as it was among the small cutlery workshops at 60 Carver Street, had close connections with Sheffield's 'little mesters'. But a *Sheffield Telegraph* article of 6 October 1964 suggested that it got its name from one of the frigates in the British Navy of the time. 'As far as I know,' a spokesman of Truswell's Brewery Co. Ltd told the newspaper, 'there has nearly always been a ship called the Royal George in the navy ... I think it does indicate that when the inn was built, Sheffield had much closer connections with the sea than it does today.' The spokesman said the Royal George was taken over by Truswells in 1871 and alterations that had been completed were the first major ones since then. A series of small rooms had been replaced by two big ones – a smoke room and a bar lounge. Principal contractors for the improvements (that had taken about a year to complete) were C. H. Gillam & Sons Ltd of Harland Road, Sheffield. Plans for the alterations were made by Hadfield, Caukwell & Davidson, chartered architects. The tenants of the house were Mr and Mrs J. W. Blake, who had been licensees of the inn for about a year. They lived in a two-storey maisonette above the ground floor, then wholly devoted to public rooms. The pub, with a history traceable to at least the 1830s, closed in 1970. The photograph was taken on 28 March 1966.

**Royal Lancers, corner of Penistone Road/Dixon Street**

During September 1984, three Sheffield pubs were put on the market by brewers Joshua Tetley, including the Royal Lancers at nos 66-68 on the Penistone Road/Dixon Street corner. Royal Lancers' landlord, Brian Howsham, said recent profits had been badly hit by losing customers through works closures, bus strikes and rising overheads. The *Star* of 10 September 1984 commented: 'The [pub dating from the 1830s and may have previously been titled Wheatsheaf] was voted one of Tetley's pubs of the year in December 1982.' Once belonging to Greaves' Norfolk Brewery, the pub eventually closed in 1985, but on 2 February 1988 the *Star* reported that plans to demolish it had been held up by Sheffield City Councillors. Planning chairman David Skinner said: 'It would be a shame to knock it down if there was a chance of refurbishing it and putting it to other uses.' And that is what eventually happened. The top picture was taken on 5 September 1984 and the one below was taken on 27 January 1988.

**Royal Standard, St Mary's Road**

Royal Standard landlord, John Williamson, revealed in 1981 that the pub, formerly belonging to William Bradley's Soho brewery, had lived with the threat of demolition since 1972. First it was to be demolished for an extension of the dual-carriageway, St Mary's Road, then later to make way for light industry. But the Royal Standard had survived in that area of upheaval while other pubs had been flattened and other buildings had fallen. John and wife Betty (pictured) were chalking up almost fourteen years there and were previously at the Bridge, Brightside. In May 1985 John boldly told the *Star* that he had reached a startling conclusion about changing drinking habits – women were downing ale faster than men: 'Times have changed. I never thought I'd be selling pints to women ... when you see one or two girls walk in you know they are going for a pint pot straightaway. They are just normal women.' The newspaper added that after thirteen years, the threat of a compulsory purchase order on his pub had been lifted, 'but he has retired and moved to Nursery Drive, Ecclesfield, before major renovation work begins.' The picture dates from 11 February 1981.

**Samuel Plimsoll, Hyde Park Flats**

Lt-Col. F. Eric Tetley, chairman of Joshua Tetley & Son Ltd, turned his hand from brewing beer to pulling pints on 17 March 1966. He marked the official opening of his company's newest pub – the Samuel Plimsoll at the Hyde Park Flats development – by pulling the first pint through the pumps. Standing by to watch that beer pipelines were in full working order was William Hatton, a former plumber with a city firm. The new pub – named after Samuel Plimsoll, inventor of the famous Plimsoll line – was the third at the huge Corporation flats development. The title 'Samuel Plimsoll' was taken for the new house, said a brewery official, because Plimsoll once worked at a Sheffield brewery – Thomas Rawson & Co. Ltd Pond Street Brewery – before moving into shipping. In fact, Plimsoll invented a very successful method of fining beer while working in Sheffield. 'His brewery was taken over by Duncan Gilmour & Company in 1946 and the latter was subsequently absorbed into the Tetley group in 1954,' said the spokesman. Managing the new house with 32-year-old William Hatton, former manager of the Lion Hotel, Nursery Street, Sheffield, was his wife Lily. The photograph was taken on 16 March 1966.

**Samuel Plimsoll Hyde Park Flats**

Interior view of the Samuel Plimsoll pub, 16 March 1966.

**Sheaf, Fraser Road, Woodseats**

The results of two years' work starting at the drawing board stage and culminating in the completion of a new £35,000 public house was seen in March 1963 when the Sheaf, in Fraser Road, Woodseats, opened its doors for the first time. Sheffield's newest pub, in one of the city's expanding suburbs, would serve the growing Fraser estate and surrounding districts. The Sheaf was a new licence for owners Joshua Tetley & Son. Landlord and landlady at the outset were Mr and Mrs Albert Petts, who were formerly at the King's Head, Darnall. Twenty-six years later, Reg Walker was one of only three surviving regulars who were present on that opening night. When the Sheaf reopened after refurbishment in July 1989, Reg, now 77, had his first pint pulled for him by Sheffield United manager Dave Bassett – the obvious guest to mark the re-opening.

**Sheaf View, Gleadless Road, Heeley**

Mike Pidgeon turned himself into a DIY expert and transformed a derelict ruin into the pub of his dreams in November 1984. Mike, aged 30 and a bachelor, had bought the dilapidated Sheaf View on Gleadless Road, Sheffield, for £20,000 eighteen months earlier. Thanks to his family who pooled their engineering and building skills, he reopened it again. After £65,000 spent and hours of back-breaking labour. His father, retired engineer Joe Pidgeon, produced a mass of detailed drawings, and his architect aunt, Anthea Hardy, turned them into reality. Completing the family connection was Mike's uncle, Sheffield University lecturer Ivan Nixon, a soil expert who gave invaluable advice. Disappointingly, during the 1990s the pub fell on hard times but once again there was another young entrepreneur who was ready to step forward and inject new life into the old building. James Birkett trained as a chef in Canada and arrived in Sheffield in 1992 to study brewing with Dave Wickett, owner of the Fat Cat and Kelham Island Brewery. Later, James made a success of the New Barrack Tavern in Penistone Road then turned his attention to the Sheaf View, securing a licence from the City magistrates to re-open the premises in December 1999. The Sheaf View may be traced as a beer house from at least the 1840s and belonged to J. L. Cockayne & Sons from 1901.

**Sheaf View, Gleadless Road, Heeley**
Pictured in August 2000 at the Sheaf View pub, Gleadless Road, Heeley, are part owner James Birkett (left) and Richard Corker (right), the pub manager.

**Shiny Sheff, junction of Crimicar Lane/Redmires Road, Lodge Moor**

The opening of the new Shiny Sheff public house on 22 April 1969 had all the appearance of a naval launching. The pub's sign-pole was decked out in bunting and the sign itself was cloaked in a Union Jack. A party of Sheffield sea cadets (pictured above) formed a guard of honour as Vice Admiral Sir John Inglis unveiled the pub sign, the Shiny Sheff. The first sod on the site was cut on 10 July 1968 by H. Murray Clarke RN, the Naval Regional Officer for the North Eastern and North Midland Region. The new pub, reported as being the fifty-first to be built by Tennant Bros since the Second World War, exploited the naval theme and included several mementos from HMS *Sheffield*, the famous wartime cruiser, scrapped in 1967, including its original nameplate and some of its stainless steel deck fittings. The bottom picture was taken on 8 May 1969.

**Shiny Sheff, junction of Crimicar Lane/ Redmires Road, Lodge Moor**

The Shiny Sheff's first licensees were Hetty and Fred Howe (pictured below) who had come to the Shiny Sheff from the Crow's Nest at Hyde Park, Sheffield. Fred served on HMS *Sheffield* in 1941 and 1942. As a mark of respect to the twenty men who died when the second HMS *Sheffield* was sunk in action during the Falklands War, the sign outside the Shiny Sheff was changed in October 1983 (shown on right). 'We used to have the WWII Shiny Sheff up there, but now it's the most recent destroyer and a map of the Falklands,' said licensee, Fred Howe.

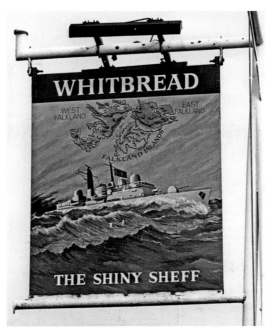

**The Sicey, Sicey Avenue, Southey Green**
Built in June 1939, the Sicey underwent extensive alterations to the tune of £160,000 early in December 1981 and re-opened as a Beefeater Steak House featuring a small 'village' within its walls. A *Star* advertising feature of 5 December 1981 gave details: 'You could spend the best part of an evening exploring the mini buildings of the olde world village, made from genuine old stone, roof tiles and other materials ... Or Annie Cummings' shop with its bow fronted window may take your fancy. A village hall which seats up to 25 people has also been included in the design. One of the main attractions is the waterfall and pond sheltering under the wide branches of a tree ... Another attraction is sure to be the live fire in the bar area. Other features range from collections of old books stacked in various nooks and crannies within the buildings, to mobile doves and owls casting a beady eye over the scene from rooftops.' Thrilled about the new venture were managers Jack and Iris Lloyd, who had been at the Sicey for more than five years.

**Sign Post, Andover Street**

The Sign Post, William Stones' new public house, opened on 7 September 1966. The premises occupied a hilly site and it was said that architects Melling & Ridgeway had used this to full advantage. The building was on three levels, with the whole of the middle level given over to the licensed premises. The official opening of the Sign Post was a happy occasion for the landlord Harry Benson, as the move had meant a return to his old neighbourhood. On 1 July 1985, the *Star* reported that Harry and Dot Benson were pulling their last pints at the pub after running it for almost twenty years.

**Sportsman Inn, Attercliffe Road**

It was new, but in a way it was old too. That was the impression people got of the new Sportsman Inn, which opened on 21 March 1958. The aim had obviously been to meet the tastes of customers who liked an old world atmosphere and those who preferred the modern appeal of a contemporary setting. 'In this the planners and the owners [S. H. Ward] had succeeded to a degree which combines delightfully the best of both,' said the *Sheffield Telegraph* of 22 March 1958.

**Sportsman, Redmires Road**

The Sportsman is pictured when Frank Taylor was the licensee under John Smith's.

**Staffordshire Arms, Sorby Street**

Staffordshire Arms landlord Wilf Hibbert and his wife were crying into their beer – alone – in February 1989. The smell from newly opened pickled onion factory next door had reduced their customers to tears and driven them from the pub in Sorby Street. Takings were down £400 a week so Wilf, 45, was kicking up a stink by calling in health experts. 'I used to like onions but not anymore,' he said. The premises were formerly part of the Chambers' Brunswick Brewery and sold to Stones' in 1912.

### Staniforth Arms, Staniforth Road

'Animal farm has come to Attercliffe … The first hint of the unusual for the visitor to the Staniforth Arms was the sight of two goats quietly grazing outside. But for landlord David Bacon it was more of a case of My Family and Other Animals,' reported the *Star* on 9 December 1989. In and around his pub David had two Alsatian dogs, two cats, two ducks, two pythons, one parrot, one cockatiel, one crow and a tarantula spider called Harry. 'The trouble is I am a soft touch for the animal down on its luck,' said David. 'I love all animals and cannot bear to hear about them suffering.' When not looking after his pub he was a children's clown known as Professor Potty and a fire-eater comedian.

### Staniforth Arms, Staniforth Road

The road with no pub made up for its deficiency on 12 November 1959 with the opening of the Staniforth Arms. For years, residents of Staniforth Road had to seek their evening's entertainment in other districts – all because of a will. The story allegedly went back to the nineteenth century when the land was owned by the Staniforth family. John Staniforth decided there would be no inns or taverns there so Staniforth Road had remained publess until 1959. The then current generation of Staniforths relented and gave Tennants Brewery permission to name the pub after the family. The first to occupy the pub were 32-year-old Eric Napier and his wife, formerly of the Broadfield Hotel, Abbeydale Road. The Staniforth Arms was designed by Husband & Co. of Glossop Road, Sheffield.

**Station Hotel, The Wicker**

In February 1969 Joshua Tetley was leading the way in the offensive against grime on the Wicker – part of Operation Spring Clean – which aimed at making Sheffield shine. Northern Gritblasters hoped to complete the job on the brewery's Station Hotel within a few days. They were using a special type of chemical developed to clean red brickwork. A spokesman for the campaign said: 'The plan to clean up the Wicker, originally drawn up by city architect, Bernard Warren, will, we think, make a tremendous impact. And the cleaning of the Station Hotel, will give the scheme a first class send off.' The Station Hotel is pictured half-way through its spring clean on 27 February 1969. Previous owners of the pub included Thomas Marrian's Burton Weir Brewery.

**Stone House, Church Street**

Featuring a courtyard bar, the Stone House was once voted one of Britain's best for its unusual decor. But in January 1986, work was to begin to give it a complete facelift. The unique bar was closed at the weekend beginning 11 January and Tetley's were to wait quite a while before they could reopen it due to a major redevelopment which prevented access from Orchard Place. When it had opened in 1971 the mock medieval courtyard was complete with pillory, olde worlde shops and a stone gatehouse modelled on York's Micklegate. The conversion of the cellar, offices and shop of the former Sheffield wine merchants White, Favell & Cockayne was the brewery's most costly one of its time.

**Stone House, Church Street**

In December 1988 it was declared that the new look Stone House, which had cost approximately £70,000, was a pub with a difference. Though the famous courtyard had gone, the ultimate in pubs with a difference was to be found in the loos where customers could listen to comedy tapes. Tetley retail area manager Tony Hector said they thought it would make a change to listen to Hancock instead of taped music. The refurbished pub was to be run by Phil and Cath Short. The picture below showing the interior was taken on 13 December 1988.

## Stones Cannon Brewery, Neepsend

William Stones and Joseph Watts went into partnership establishing the Cannon Brewery, Acorn Street, in 1849. The brewery name may have come from the nearby foundry that cast gun barrels. Following Watts' death in 1854, Stones continued brewing by himself. In 1868 he purchased the lease of the Neepsend Brewery and renamed it the Cannon Brewery after his original premises. He continued to brew there until his death in 1894. In 1912, Stones acquired the houses of Chambers' Brunswick Brewery. More significantly, in 1954 Stones took over Mappins of Rotherham. Stones Bitter was brewed at the Cannon Brewery from 1948 and was popular with Sheffield's steel workers. In 1968 William Stones amalgamated with Bass Charrington. Stones Bitter was originally available across the south of Yorkshire, Derbyshire and Nottinghamshire, with distribution extended to the rest of the north of England in 1977, and nationwide from 1979, accompanied by a considerable marketing push. The picture below was taken on 18 January 1990 and depicts Stones Brewery Manager Reg Bird.

**Stones Cannon Brewery, Neepsend**

Increasing demand saw Stones Bitter also brewed at other Bass breweries from the 1970s onwards. The beer's popularity reached its apex in 1992 when it was the country's highest selling bitter, selling 240 million pints. The beer has been lauded in certain quarters as 'one of Sheffield's most famous exports'. Stones notably sponsored the Rugby Football League Championship and its successor, the Rugby Super League, from 1986 until 1997. A well-known series of television advertisements for the brand, starring Tony Barton and Michael Angelis, became the longest running bitter advertisements in the country, extending from 1983 until 1991. Bass closed the Cannon Brewery in April 1999 with the loss of fifty-seven jobs. A year later the company sold its brewing operations to the Belgian brewer Interbrew who were ordered by the Competition Commission to sell the Stones brand. In 2002, the brand was purchased by the American Coors Brewing Company, who merged to become Molson Coors in 2005. In the top picture the brewery is seen on 18 January 1990. On the same date, in the photograph below, workers are seen in the fermenting room skimming the yeast from the vessel tops.

**Surrey and Fringe, Surrey Street**

The Lord Mayor of Sheffield opened the Surrey and Fringe, a new pub and health club complex in the city on 4 December 1984. Councillor Roy Munn arrived at the Surrey Street development in a horse-drawn surrey, but when he adjourned to the downstairs bar he betrayed a feeling that while the swish surroundings might be alright for some folk, they were not his pint of ale. Representatives of Mansfield Brewery, who had sunk £750,000 in the project, were quick to point out that their lager had won top awards. Councillor Munn also revealed that if he had had his way a few years earlier, Mansfield would never have got their hands on the premises. 'When I was deputy chairman of the libraries and arts committee, we were looking at a possible Sheffield home for the Ruskin collection. If it had been up to me, we would have used the building as a Ruskin gallery but I was over-ruled.'

### Target Inn, Hyde Park

On 8 September 1965 the *Sheffield Telegraph* reported that the Hyde Park development was to have a new pub of a modern design and character to compliment the new flats. The Target Inn was one of two pubs that brewery S. H. Wards & Co. Ltd. were opening in Sheffield's new housing developments, the other being the Bathfield in Netherthorpe. The Target Inn replaced a pub of the same name located in St John's Road, which had been lost to the flats, and the new pub was to have a full licence. A distinguishing feature of the pub was to be a mural by Mr Dick Rainer, a lecturer at Sheffield College of Art. Mr and Mrs Barry Chaplin were to be the first managers. Seventeen years later Ward's Brewery had to call for reinforcements after the beer delivery to the Target Inn, Hyde Park, came under attack in 'bomb alley'. The *Star* of 7 August 1982 said that the brewery had added a third man to the delivery so he could watch for missiles being thrown from the balconies. The move came after a number of close calls in recent months.

### Target Inn, Hyde Park

On 9 August 1982, the *Star* said that landlord Brian Norfolk (pictured) was refusing to pay his rates to Sheffield Council in an attempt to make them take action over the constant barrage of missiles that rained down on the pub. The latest items included a TV stand and baby walker. Mr Norfolk said: 'It's the only way to get them to take notice. I want all this lot stopping before someone gets hit on the head.' The council had set up a meeting to try to address the problem.

### Three Cranes, Queen Street

The *Star* of 24 January 1980 noted that four men had to be ejected from the Three Cranes pub, Queen Street. The men in question were members of the Hallam Constituency Labour Party and were drinking in the pub after a meeting of the Hallam general management committee. Landlord George Butler asked the men to drink up and leave but one refused and police were called. The men indicated that their ejection was politically motivated as one said: 'he [the landlord] is obviously not a Labour Party sympathiser.' The men were to write to magistrates to object to the renewal of the landlord's licence and Labour Councillor David Brown said: 'There was no need for him to act in this high-handed attitude'. Mr Butler commented: 'There was nothing really in it at all. It was nothing to do with their politics.' The Three Cranes can be traced to at least 1822 and was part of Truswell's tied estate from 1860.

### Three Feathers, Bowden Wood, Prince of Wales Road

The Three Feathers, Bowden Wood Crescent, was the host of an unusual scientific experiment in December 1972. Twelve people were allowed to drink as much as they liked to show how their eyesight was affected as the level of alcohol in their blood rose. The experiment was directed by the road safety section of the City Engineer's Department. One of the participants, Maurice Stamford said: 'I love drinking. I can hold my own with anybody. I wish this thing happened more often.' Maurice added that he did not drive because he drank. The results showed that vision was affected by about 10 per cent with clarity and field of vision the most adversely affected. As a result of the experiment, the bill was left to be paid for by Wards Brewery. Both pictures date from 3 February 1958; the pub opened a day later. The licence of the new building was the one transferred from the Stafford Arms, Duke Street, which was demolished at the beginning of 1957 to make way for the flats.

### Three Tuns Hotel, Leopold Street

Regulars of the Three Tuns Hotel, Leopold Street, drank the pub dry along with other customers on its final night on 11 September 1985. The Three Tuns, dating from at least 1822, was closing as part of the Fargate redevelopment, which would see the area transformed into a shopping and pedestrian precinct. The writing was on the wall, literally, as the regulars left messages and jokes during the farewell party, which saw the supply of lager, cider and beer exhausted. It was the end of an era for some of the older patrons, especially one who had been going to the pub for seventy-one years. Landlord Paul Jones said: 'There will be a lot of our elder lunchtime and afternoon regulars who will be very disappointed. They're saying they don't know where they will go. We feel rather sorry for them.' Paul and landlady Barbara Jones were going to the Gallows, Dinnington. The picture dates from 15 December 1975.

**Tut 'n' Shive (Dove & Rainbow), Hartshead**
Kathy Askew is pictured behind the Tut 'n' Shive bar on 25 November 1993.

**Tut 'n' Shive (Dove and Rainbow), Hartshead**
Refurbishment work at the Dove & Rainbow, which turned the pub into the Tut 'n' Shive, left customers bemused as to whether the work had actually been completed and if the brewery had employed some 'cowboy' builders. The changes were intentional and were a part of a new look envisaged by owners Whitbread's Brewery. The company's Sherwood Inns area manager Andy Mills told the *Star* of 29 August 1992: 'Pubs nowadays are increasingly looking the same – we have created one that is about theatre and gives a lot of interest.' The new decor consisted of a bar made from old bits of doors, a piece of scaffolding for the bar footrail and the ceiling was a collage of corrugated iron sheeting, old doors and pieces of discarded wallpaper. Half of an old caravan was also used as a partition wall between the kitchen and bar. This transformation was part of a larger scheme of refurbishments in the South Yorkshire area with pubs in Doncaster and Rotherham similarly altered. One feature of those alterations which was not transferred to the Tut 'n' Shive in Sheffield was the use of toilet seats for chairs. The pub proudly announced on an outdoor sign: 'Our toilets are IN the toilet.'

**Viaduct, The Wicker**

In the past there have been two incidents in the early hours of the morning concerning the Viaduct pub on the Wicker. In May 1986 landlord Alan Fearnley and his family were asleep as fire raged at the pub, which he had taken only three weeks previously. An unknown passer-by saw flames and raised the alarm. 'We are very grateful. Without the warning we might not have got out alive,' said landlady Lesley Fearnley. At 1.15 a.m. early in December 1999, Viaduct landlady Linda Ryder, 37, tried to help an apparent robbery victim but ended up facing a terrifying ordeal herself. She opened the front door when a tearful woman claimed to have been mugged. But on doing so she found the woman was with a thug who thumped her in the face. The man then threatened to 'find her kids' who were asleep upstairs unless she opened the safe. Linda already recovering from a burglary the previous week, was forced to open the safe and the raiders snatched hundreds of pounds in takings. Her children Deana, aged 16, and Robert, 9, slept through. 'It's noisy here and they have got used to sleeping through it. I have never seen [the woman or the man] before, but they knew enough about me to know I was here with my kids,' she said. The premises date from at least the 1850s and were formerly tied to Whitmarsh, Watson & Company's South Street Brewery.

**Victoria Hotel, Penistone Road**

In July 1961 the Victoria Hotel on Penistone Road was looking forward to the completion of a replanning and redecoration scheme which had begun some months earlier. Ron Nash, who rented the hotel from Tennant Bros, said the living quarters for himself and his family had been moved entirely to the first floor, toilets moved inside and the three existing rooms all provided with brand new bars and redecorated throughout. Ron's wife Beryl was one of the youngest landladies in Sheffield. They both took over the hotel from Ron's father in 1958. Beryl is pictured in one of the bars at the re-styled hotel in 1961.

**Victoria Hotel, Penistone Road**

Exterior view of the Victoria Hotel on Penistone Road, 4 March 1986. The pub, which dates from at least 1855, was formerly tied to Thomas Berry's Moorhead Brewery.

### Victoria Hotel, Penistone Road

Sadly, in 1986, bulldozers called time on Ron Nash's dream of being a one-pub man. A road widening scheme meant that it was last orders at the Victoria Hotel on 5 March 1986. 'We've had a great life here,' said Ron as he recalled circus lion cubs in the bar, comedian Charlie Williams calling regularly for a swift half, international football stars from Germany, Spain and Switzerland coming in for meals during the 1966 World Cup. Then there was the market trader called Bob who walked up to the bar and handed Ron and his wife two tickets to Majorca, just to say 'thank you.' The Owls used to have their Christmas parties at the Vic as did local pensioners, steelworkers from Richard Carr and sweetmakers from Bassetts. The food was legendary. 'I did the catering which I've always loved and Beryl was always the gaffer in the bar,' said Ron. 'If I had my time again, I wouldn't change a thing,' added Beryl who managed to bring up three children in her spare time. After the closure the couple moved to the Lady Bridge pub in the city centre and then to the Peacock at Stannington before retiring in January 1995. The couple are pictured here on 4 March 1986.

### Vulcan, Northern Avenue

When the Vulcan opened on 20 May 1969 it boasted good beer and something else besides – one of the best panoramic views of the city from a picture window along one wall of the lounge bar. It was 10 yards long and as high as the room wall. The view stretched out across the city towards the North West. 'It must be one of the best views to be seen from any bar in Sheffield,' said John Tate, Sheffield area manager for John Smith's, owners of the Vulcan. The pub was only the second one in Sheffield – city of steel – to be named after the Roman god of fire and metal workers. The other was called the Vulcan Tavern. But though the name Vulcan was appropriate for a Sheffield public house, it also had its problems, as was discovered when it was decided to decorate the back of the bar with a Vulcan motif – Vulcan is traditionally shown completely nude. 'It was thought a bit unsuitable for a place where there are men and women together, so he has been made decent,' said John Tate. First licensee of the new Vulcan was Reginald Watson; born and bred in Sheffield, he had spent the previous two years at the Strad Hotel on the Stradbroke estate.

**Waggon & Horses, Abbeydale Road**

The Waggon & Horses pub football team had an unlikely new player for their tour of Malta, the *Star* reported on 28 April 1983. He was none other than England, Stoke and Blackpool legend Sir Stanley Matthews. He was to play for half an hour against Maltese side Sliema Wanderers as he was a resident on the island. The pub team had organised four matches for the tour, with some of their opponents taking part in the following season's European cup competition. Organiser of the tour, Norman Parkin, told the paper: 'It's going to be a real experience for the lads. The Maltese are dead keen on football and are keen to beat whoever they meet, and it will be great for the team when Stan Matthews turns out alongside them.' The exterior view of the pub was taken on 25 February 1974.

**Waggon & Horses, Abbeydale Road**

In November 1993 it was announced that the Waggon & Horses was the latest member of the Tom Cobleigh pub chain following in the footsteps of two other Sheffield pubs; the Old Queen's Head and the Ridgeway Arms. The Waggon & Horses had undergone a £750,000 refurbishment to bring it in line with the Tom Cobleigh style of decoration. Presiding over the premises were managers Steve and Shirley Conway, who had ten years in the trade. Steve had previously spent nine years as a professional footballer with Sheffield United.

**Waggon & Horses, Gleadless Road**

Terry Warwick, former landlord of the Waggon & Horses, Gleadless Road, was hoping that the pub's resident ghost had not taken such a liking to him and that it would follow him to his new job at the Railway Hotel, Blackburn, in June 1981. The *Star* said that Terry had been at the Waggon & Horses for five years and experienced a number of unexplained events. These included barrels rolling around the cellar, footsteps being heard in empty rooms, lights turned on and off, and his wife Diane felt eyes watching her. The photograph dates from 14 March 1988.

**Weetwood House, Ecclesall Road**

Formerly Ecclesall library, Weetwood House, was refurbished by pub chain Tom Cobleigh at a cost of £2.3 million in 1995 to become their flagship premises. The refurbishment was done in keeping with the area and the history of the building, with the only new addition to the premises being a conservatory. In 1998, Weetwood House was converted to be solely a restaurant catering for retired people. The pub was later sold to developers and Weetwood Gardens housing development now stands on the site. The photograph was taken on 24 January 1996.

### Wellington, Brightside

In April 1995, landlord of the Wellington, Thomas Farley, was considering demanding compensation from Sheffield Development Corporation after roadworks were causing his custom to fall considerably. The work was for the new Don Valley link road and he said he had been affected for over a year. Mr Farley said the last straw was when workers digging outside the pub left a gaping hole which blocked off the entrance to the car park causing customers to think again about stopping for refreshment.

He added: 'There's nowhere to park, the windows vibrate and there's the noise from the JCBs.' A spokesman for the Sheffield Development Corporation said: 'We apologise for any disruption and will do our best to complete the work within a week.' The pub has since been demolished.

### Wellington, Brightside

In 1986 tenant Keith Taylor called it a day at the Wellington pub in Brightside as he said he had lost £10,000 in five years. Owners William Stones said that they would not close the pub but were considering its future. The pub was located next to Forgemasters steel works and the decline of the steel industry was a major factor in the pub's decline. Mr Taylor said: 'I have seen the workforce dwindle at the nearby River Don works until now it is little more than a thousand.'

**West End Hotel, Glossop Road**

Bar staff at the West End Hotel were getting into the charity spirit reported the *Star* of 25 October 1977. Dave Scott, barman at the pub, was going to slim down from his 15 stone figure to raise money for a muscular dystrophy charity. Dave, who said he drank 100 pints a week, was calling time on the challenge before the Christmas period, however, so he could enjoy the celebrations. His target weight was 12 stones and he was planning to cut down on the pints, fatty foods and take up rugby training. Dave said: 'I'm afraid my weight is an occupational hazard but if I can lose weight up until Christmas I can have a few then and enjoy myself.' Two girls from the pub, Julia and Karen Theaker, were also raising money for the same charity by walking from Sheffield to Doncaster. The pub dates from at least 1852 and became part of Thomas Rawson & Company's Pond Street Brewery in 1855. The photograph was taken on 16 March 1966.

**Wharncliffe Hotel, Beavercotes Road**

Plans for a youth bar serving soft drinks in the basement of the Wharncliffe Hotel, Firth Park, were rejected by a Department of the Environment inspector after an appeal by Whitbread's Brewery in November 1981. The idea caused a stir and the story featured quite prominently over a period in the columns of the *Star*. Residents had objected to the plans saying they feared it would increase noise, petty crime and vandalism in the area. The police supported the idea in principle but did not want the scheme in the middle of a residential suburb where it would lead to friction and disturb local people. The pub dates from the late 1920s and the photograph was taken on 4 November 1981.

**Wheatsheaf, Parkhead**

The *Sheffield Telegraph* of 30 April 1984 reported that the Wheatsheaf pub, Parkhead, had quite an unusual customer. It was not 49-year-old former barrister and SAS major Rex Blaker, it was his companion, Rattus Japonicus, also known as Steve, the Japanese hooded rat. They often popped into the pub for a quick pint during the evening and the other patrons were free to stroke Steve, which was a frequent request. During the day Rex was a lecturer in property law at Sheffield Polytechnic but was frequently mistaken for a Hell's Angel due to his evening attire of fringed motorbiking jacket.

**Whispers, Carlisle Road**

The *Star* of 31 October 1985 proudly announced that Europe's first video bar was set to open in Sheffield the following day. Whispers was the new identity of the once derelict Carwood that had undergone an £80,000-plus revamp. The project was reportedly backed by Scottish & Newcastle Brewery, Sheffield DJ Spider Watson and Derby colleague John Kay. About sixteen video screens were being installed in the twin-level venue and the partners believed it was the first in Europe.

**White Hart, Worksop Road**

The photograph was taken on 4 November 1981.

**White Lion, Barker's Pool**

Dating back to the late eighteenth century, the White Lion is depicted when Charles Arch was the licensee and it was tied to Thomas Rawson & Company's Pond Street Brewery. Parry (1997) states the pub was formerly called the Well Run Dimple.

**Yorkshire Grey, Charles Street**

Landlord Bill Stanaway believed in old-fashioned values and he reckoned there were enough Sheffield folk of the same mind to support the venture he launched on 2 April 1984. At that time he was President of the Sheffield & District LVA; he celebrated his fifth anniversary in the licensed trade by launching a new venture which turned the clock back from fun pub to traditional tavern. Consequently, the former Bar Rio on city centre Charles Street, once the Minerva Tavern, became the Victorian-style pub, The Yorkshire Grey. Whitbread, deciding the fun pub had outlived its usefulness, opted for a drastic change and Bill said: 'Standards come before gimmicks. We believe the Victorians had it right ... It is a strike against the plastic world. I wanted to go back to wood – that's why we have real mahogany in the pub.'